OVER 100 HEARTY, WHOLESOME RECIPES FOR BEANS OF EVERY KIND, PREPARED IN TRUE AMERICAN STYLE

OTHER BOOKS BY F. H. "TED" WASKEY

THE PROFESSIONAL FOOD BUYER,
WITH M. C. WARFEL

THE MODERN ESCOFFIER

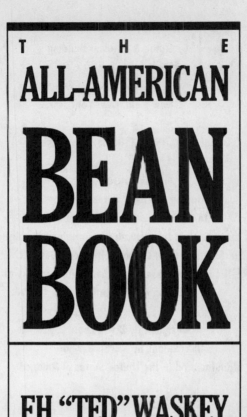

THE ALL-AMERICAN BEAN BOOK

F.H. "TED" WASKEY

ILLUSTRATIONS BY MARTIN BERMAN

A FIRESIDE BOOK
PUBLISHED BY SIMON & SCHUSTER
NEW YORK   LONDON   TORONTO
SYDNEY   TOKYO   SINGAPORE

Fireside
Simon & Schuster Building
Rockefeller Center
1230 Avenue of the Americas
New York, New York 10020

Designed by Bonni Leon
Illustrations by Martin Berman
Manufactured in the United States of America

5   7   9   10   8   6

Library of Congress Cataloging in Publication Data

Waskey, Frank H.
The all American bean book / F. H. "Ted" Waskey;
illustrations by Martin Berman.
p.   cm.
Includes index.
1. Cookery (Beans)   2. Cookery, American.   I. Title.
TX803.B4W37   1988
641.6'565—dc 19   88-16571
ISBN 0-671-64403-3

TO CLAIRE

ACKNOWLEDGMENTS

The following organizations and persons have generously contributed their time and expertise in aiding the author in bean cookery and research:

The Idaho Bean Commission, 212 Continental Life Building, Boise Idaho, for bean research and some of the recipes.

Dr. Philip S. Chen, Ph.D., author of *Soybeans for Health, Longevity and Economy,* published by Chemical Elements Publishers, Atlantic Union College, South Lancaster, Massachusetts.

Thomas Kennedy, Michigan Bean Company, Saginaw, Michigan.

Henry O. Klein, 311 California Street, San Francisco, California.

Gordon W. Monfort, California Lima Bean Advisory Board, Los Angeles, California.

Ella Lehr Nisja, Home Economics Services, Idaho Bean Commission.

Mama Marcy Rossi, Paradise, California, for kitchen testing.

Messrs. Warren Piwetz, Earl J. (Chip) Mitchell, and David Rich, Undergraduates in Mechanical Engineering, Cullen College of Engineering, The University of Houston, University Park, Texas.

The Blackeyed Pea Council of the California Dry Bean Advisory Board, and the Board itself, Dinuba, California.

Professor Kathleen Zolber, Ph.D., R.D., Director of Nutrition and Dietetics, School of Allied Health, The Loma Linda University, Loma Linda, California, and Past President of the American Dietetic Association.

Professor Marilyn Chou, Director, The Food Advisory Board and Consultant, The Hudson Institute.

Dr. Louis Lazaroff, Director, General, The International Council of Development of Underutilized Plants, Orinda, California, for his help in identifying and writing about the "Winged Bean."

Maxine Isert, Soy Nutrition Specialist, Soy Oil Programs, The American Soybean Association, St. Louis, Missouri.

The Soy Protein Council, Washington, D.C.

Professor Douglas R. Buck, Ph.D.,R.D., Wethersfield, Connecticut.

Red River Edible Bean Growers Association, Frazee, Minnesota.

Rocky Mountain Bean Dealers Association, Denver, Colorado.

Michigan Bean Commission, Lansing, Michigan.

Dr. Joseph Rackis, USDA Northern Regional Research Center, Peoria, Illinois.

Mr. Truett Airhart, Truett's, Inc., P.O. Box 770174, Houston, Texas, for his permission to use the International Chili Contest Winning recipes.

Mr. Herbert Wilson, Executive Vice President, The Texas Hotel & Motel Association, San Antonio, Texas, for permission to publish his favorite chili recipe.

Mr. W.H. "Buckshot" Price, Executive Vice President, The Texas Restaurant Association, Austin, Texas, for the four recipes that he picked out as being, in his professional judgment, some of the "best ever" chili recipes.

The late Mr. Joe E. Cooper, for the knowledge gained in reading his *With Or Without Beans*, published in 1952 by William S. Henson, Inc.

The late Honorable U.S. Senator Everett Dirksen, for his "Homage to the Bean."

CONTENTS

HOMAGE TO THE BEAN

It was many years ago that a very dignified and slightly belligerent senator took himself to the Senate Dining Room to order bean soup, only to discover that there was no bean soup on the menu. This dereliction on the part of Senate Dining Room cooks called for an immediate declaration of war. So the senator promptly introduced a resolution to the effect that henceforth not a day should pass, when the Senate was in session and the restaurant open, that there would not be bean soup on the menu. It has, therefore, become an inviolate practice and a glorious tradition that the humble little bean should always be honored.

There is much to be said for the succulent little bean —any kind of a bean, be it kidney, navy, green, wax, Kentucky, chili, baked, pinto, Mexican, or any other kind. Not only is it high in nourishment, but is particularly rich in that nutritious value referred to as protein—the stuff that imparts energy and drive to the bean eater and particularly the senators who need this sustaining force when they prepare for a long speech on the Senate floor.

I venture the belief that the marathon speakers of the Senate going back as far as the day of the celebrated "Kingfish," Senator Huey Pierce Long of Louisiana, and coming down to the modern marathoners in the forensic art such as Senator Strom Thurmond of South Carolina and Senator Wayne Morse of Oregon, both of whom have spoken well in excess of twenty hours and felt no ill effects, would agree the little bean had much to do with this sustained torrent of oratory.

In my enumeration of the bean varieties, I forgot to include one of the most celebrated of all beans, namely, the soybean. Not only has this little Oriental produce sustained a civilization in China for perhaps thousands of years, but it has been broken down into so many components that, like Atlas, it fairly carries the weight of the world on its tiny little shoulders. The soybean today produces soya cake for cattle feed, which is highly prized by dairymen and beef producers. Its oils are used for preparing table spreads and cooking oils. It is low in unsaturated fats and is prized by dietitians and that vast host who devote so much of a lifetime to keeping a svelte figure. Its oils are further broken down for use in house paints and the soya cake can now be compressed so hard that it makes door handles and gadgetry without number.

Some day some historical bonepicker seeking a subject for a world-shaking thesis that will live as long as Shakespeare will hit upon the lowly bean. What a welter of knowledge he will develop in his research, and I am sure he will come to the conclusion that without the bean, the earth would have long slipped into orbit and disappeared among a galaxy inhabited by bean eaters. Hail to the bean!

By the late Senator Everett Dirksen,
Written at the request of the late Victor Bennett in 1966

FOREWORD

Beans have probably fed more hungry people than any food known to man. Disdained for centuries by certain classes of society as a poor man's meal, and considered by many farmers to be a fickle crop, requiring infinite growing care, the bean today occupies an honored place in the world's food basket.

In fact, beans are one of the oldest and most universally used foods. They have been traced back to the Bronze Age in Switzerland. They were a favorite food among the early Greeks and their Trojan rivals, as we know from evidence found in the ruins of Ilium. So popular were beans in ancient Egypt that it is said temples were dedicated to them, where the bean was worshiped as a symbol of life itself. Among the early Jews, beans were eaten one thousand years before the dawn of the Christian era. The Romans, famous for their feasting, used beans extensively and even gambled with them. Most authorities agree that beans were grown in South America by the ancient Peruvian natives.

The Jews of North Africa baked beans every Friday to eat on Saturday, the Jewish Sabbath, when religious observance prohibits all work, including cooking. The same motive impelled the early settlers in New England. Throughout the Northeast, Saturday ovens were laden with bean pots to supply Saturday supper, Sunday breakfast or dinner, or any combination of the three. It is likely that the early Massachusetts colonists learned the gentle art of bean baking from the local Indians, who used earthenware pots and may have sweetened the beans with maple syrup before the advent of molasses.

Historians tell us that warfare introduced beans to much of the world; they were carried by ancient armies as a staple among the fighting rations of soldiers on the march. Our own Teddy Roosevelt said he won the Battle of San Juan Hill on beans. During World War II, our army floated waterproof bags of beans from ships to beach-heads.

Beans are a valuable source of food wherever transportation is a problem. Their low water content and high vitamin and protein rating make them inexpensive relative to their nutritional value. Because they store easily and are relatively nonperishable, beans are a compact source of energy at low cost.

For those of us who limit our bean cookery to baked beans and black bean soup (both, very likely, from cans), it may take a leap of the imagination to look beyond Boston baked beans with catsup and brown bread for Saturday night supper, or past that bowl of bean soup, black as your hat, garnished with pale lemon slices. But there is much more to bean cookery than these two cherished dishes.

The chili con carne and frijoles of Mexico and the American Southwest, hopping John of the South, and red beans and rice of old New Orleans are examples of some of the most popular national and regional dishes that have delighted the palates of generations of Americans.

There is no end to the versatility of the bean. From a thrifty family meal to fancy party fare; from delicious hors d'oeuvres to soups, salads, and casseroles; from formal occasions to snacks or barbecues—the bean has no peer among foods in the hands of an imaginative cook.

This book had its inception in Victor Bennett's fertile mind way back in the early 1960s. But it is most appropriate that it has come into fruition now, when we see the evidence that "gourmet dining" leads to less than optimum health and when research has finally discovered a verifiable, causative relationship between, for instance, coronary heart disease and cholesterol intake. For those who wish to vary their traditional eating styles and habits, either for a change from everyday, humdrum meals, or in the quest for more healthful living patterns, this book will serve as a source of inspiration and information.

The All-American Bean Book is not a "diet book," nor do I believe that a completely vegetarian regime is the Holy Grail to be sought by every health-conscious individual. In fact, about half of my recipes call for meat, fish, or chicken used in combination with beans. However, for those who, because of religious, clinical, or personal reasons, wish to try either a lacto-ovo (no meat) or vegan (no meat or dairy products) diet, there are plenty of recipes to suit their tastes and purposes.

Ted Waskey

THE BEAN AND NUTRITION

THE CASE AGAINST FATTY FOODS

A large body of scientific studies have documented a correlation between fat intake and coronary heart disease. Generally, experts agree that if one's dietary intake of fats is "prudent"—to borrow the American Heart Association's term—and mostly from unsaturated fat sources, chances of developing heart disease will lessen.

In 1970 the report of the Senate Select Committee on Nutrition was issued by the government. Carried out under the auspices of the National Heart, Lung, and Blood Institute, the study established definitively that there is a causative link between dietary fats and coronary heart disease.

These were the major conclusions of this landmark report: (1) Heart disease is directly connected to the level of cholesterol in the blood. (2) By lowering one's blood cholesterol, one reduces the incidence of fatal heart attacks. (3) The more one lowers cholesterol and fat in the diet, the more one reduces one's risk of heart disease.

Until this study was published, a blood cholesterol level

of 265 was considered "safe." But the report suggested that a level of 210 or less would prove beneficial in preventing coronary heart disease. Finally, for the first time, the government recommended "dietary intervention [as] the first line of attack," and Americans at last began to take their diets seriously.

With the new consciousness of what food means to our present and future health, we have begun to eat with more awareness. Understanding which foods contain large amounts of saturated fats and cholesterol is an important step.

As most of us know by now, eggs and red meats have the highest cholesterol levels, followed by dairy products and then fish, with *no* cholesterol showing in oils at all. Among saturated fats, we have much the same story: dairy products, red meats, and eggs top the list, with saturated fats from coconut and palm oils showing slightly higher fat contents than fish and seafood. Finally, cheese, because it is a concentrated food, contains more fat and cholesterol per unit measure than other foods do.

WHY WE SHOULD EAT BEANS

Legumes, except for soybeans, are very low in any kind of fat (and what fat they do have is unsaturated), and they contain no cholesterol at all. By substituting beans for part of the animal or dairy protein in your diet, you can eliminate some of the saturated fats and cholesterol that might contribute to your chances of getting coronary heart disease. It is often said that the protein consumed in most legumes is not complete protein; that is, the amino-acid balance in dried beans makes them less efficient as protein than the amino acid balance in eggs and beef, which are considered complete proteins. However

if beans and peas are served with a complementary food
—any grain, green vegetables. nuts, cheese, eggs, meat,
poultry, or fish—the combination of the two foods will
result in a complete protein from which full nutritional
benefit will be derived.

OTHER REASONS WHY BEANS ARE BENEFICIAL

- Beans are high in protein: one cup of cooked beans
  will supply about one-third the RDA for protein.
- Beans are high in fiber: meat, poultry, fish, eggs, and
  dairy products contain *no* dietary fiber.
- Beans are high in most vitamins and minerals except
  for vitamin C, in which they are totally deficient, and
  vitamin A, in which they are either exceptionally low
  or totally deficient.

Recent findings have shown that a high-fiber diet is one
of the means of preventing cancer of the colon. Because
beans are a wonderful source of crude fiber, they are at
the head of the class of foods that can be used effectively
in the body's fight against cancer. Furthermore, during
the process of elimination, the crude fiber in beans sops
up water and this water-ladened waste, on its way to the
lower bowel, gives the eater a sense of extra fullness,
which can delay the next onset of hunger pangs or other
"eating triggers."

Research has also shown that the presence of ade-
quate fiber in the diet can help control blood cholesterol
and glucose levels. A high glucose level in the blood can
adversely affect people with diabetes. They, and people
who suffer from hypoglycemia (low blood sugar levels),
find that the carbohydrates in beans do not trigger as
high a level of insulin response as do the carbohydrates

in other starchy foods, such as potatoes and grain products. New studies indicate that every time the body secretes insulin to control an increase in blood sugar, more of that blood sugar tends to be stored as body fat. Because beans provoke a lower insulin response, they are a more beneficial food for diabetics than other starchy carbohydrates as well as a perfect low-fat protein substitute.

Because of their high carbohydrate content, dried beans and peas have been categorized by weight-conscious dieters as fattening food that must be avoided in the quest for a high-energy, low-calorie regime. However, compared calorie for calorie with most red meat and cheese, beans, provided they are not liberally doused with fat and sweeteners, are a superb protein for people who must control their weight.

HOW ABOUT GAS?

Everyone has felt the discomfort of gas. In beans, the problem arises from three sugarlike compounds—raffinose, stachyose, and verbacose—that the body cannot transform into usable substances, as it does with other sugars. Instead, these compounds are passed along to the large intestine where they are broken down into gases, about 95 percent of them colorless and odorless, although they may cause some discomfort from bloating. Unfortunately, about 5 percent of the gases cause flatulence.

This problem can be mitigated to some extent in your cooking preparations: first, soak the beans in plenty of water, using either the short or long soaking methods described on pages 17 and 18, then discard the soaking liquid and rinse the beans well under running water before you cook them in fresh liquid.

THE BEAN POT

A FEW HELPFUL HINTS ABOUT COOKING BEANS

SOAKING

It is necessary to soak dried beans before cooking them in order to return the water lost in drying. (Lentils and dried peas, however, need not be soaked.)

LONG METHOD.   Spread the beans out on a flat surface and pick them over to remove any pebbles, leaves, or twigs. Place the beans in a strainer and rinse them under cold running water. Put them in a container with a generous quantity of water and let the beans stand for at least 4 or 5 hours or overnight. Drain the beans, discard the soaking liquid, and rinse the beans again under running water. Cook the beans as directed below or in a recipe.

SHORT METHOD.   Pick over and rinse the beans as

described above. Place the beans in a saucepan, add fresh water to cover them by several inches, and cover the pan. Bring the water to a boil, remove the pan from the heat, and let the beans soak for 1 to 2 hours. Drain and rinse the beans as instructed above.

COOKING THE BEANS

STOVETOP METHOD. Place the soaked beans in a saucepan, preferably a heavy one because the beans will have to simmer for a long time, and the heavier the pan the less likely it is that they will scorch. Cover the beans with cold water, using at least 3 times as much water as there are beans, and bring them to a boil over high heat. Lower the heat and simmer the beans, covered, until they are tender. It is important that the beans simmer as they cook; if they boil rapidly their skins will break more easily and the beans will mush up. Add water to the pot from time to time if the liquid seems too low and the beans appear to be in danger of sticking to the bottom of the pan.

PRESSURE COOKER METHOD. Place the soaked beans in the pressure cooker, add at least 3 times as much water as there are beans and 1 tablespoon or so of butter, drippings, or vegetable oil, depending on how you plan to use the beans—the oil will help keep the foam from bubbling up too high. Cover the pot and cook the beans at 15 pounds of pressure as follows: split peas and lentils, 10 to 12 minutes; all other beans 15 to 20 minutes; except soybeans and garbanzos, 25 to 30 minutes.

SALT

Add salt only after the beans are soft, otherwise the salt will toughen the bean and prevent its becoming tender.

THE
BEAN
POT

Most of my recipes call for adding salt to taste, but another rule of thumb is 1 teaspoon of salt for each cup of dried beans. Adjust this amount downward, however, if salty meat, such as bacon or ham hocks, is part of the dish.

TOMATOES AND TOMATO JUICE

Add these somewhat acid ingredients only after the beans are almost tender, otherwise the beans will not soften.

HARD WATER

Hard water slows down cooking and sometimes can simply stop the cooking, no matter how fast the water bubbles in the pot. If you know that your water is hard, add a scant ⅛ teaspoon of baking soda for each cup of dried beans. Too much soda will leach out flavor and nutritional value, so use only this small amount.

SERVING SIZE

As a rule, 1 pound of beans will provide 8 or 9 ¾-cup servings.

SUBSTITUTION OF INGREDIENTS

Almost any recipe in this book that contains meat can be made vegetarian. Although salt pork or some kind of salty meat seems so intrinsic to baked beans that removing it would be sacrilege, the judicious addition of other ingredients, including herbs and spices, can produce a very respectable dish. So feel free to experiment with these recipes; not only are they delicious as written (and then cooked), they can also form the basis for a whole new culinary repertoire.

Never hesitate to use fresh herbs instead of dried; their vivid flavor will intensify your pleasure in eating.

Unless you are making stuffed tomatoes (page 133) or one of the salads calling for fresh tomatoes, canned Italian plum tomatoes are an excellent substitute, especially in the dead of winter when ripe tomatoes tend to be hard as rocks and to taste like cotton batting.

Frozen vegetables are an acceptable substitute for most of the fresh ones listed in my ingredients.

CANNED DRIED BEANS

Canned beans are a valuable resource to have on hand, and they are now available in an astonishingly wide variety. Use them wherever they are appropriate; that is, where cooked beans are an ingredient, or where the beans cook without any other vegetables or flavorings. Drain canned beans in a colander and rinse them quickly under running water to wash off as much salt as possible.

And now it is time for you to embark on the Great American Bean Adventure.

SPREADS, DIPS, AND OTHER APPETIZERS

REFRIED BEAN DIP

1 cup refried
beans (page
121), chilled

1 cup sour cream

1 tablespoon
bottled salsa
jalapeña

• 2 CUPS

■ Mash the beans thoroughly in a bowl with a fork, or use the food processor. Add the sour cream and salsa and blend the dip until smooth. Serve with tortilla chips, corn chips, or crackers.

BAKED BEAN SPREAD

1 cup homemade
(pages 138 to 146)
or canned baked
beans, chilled

2 teaspoons finely
chopped chives

2 tablespoons
vegetable oil

1 teaspoon finely
chopped fresh
parsley

Dash hot
pepper sauce

1 teaspoon fresh
lemon or lime
juice

Salt

■ In a bowl with a fork, or in a food processor, mash the beans to a smooth purée. Stir in the chives, parsley, oil, lemon juice, hot pepper sauce, and salt to taste. Blend well and chill the mixture before serving with crackers or toast.

• 1 CUP

BAKED BEAN
SANDWICH SPREADS

■ Save a cup or so of any of our spectacular baked bean recipes (pages 138 to 146), or use canned baked beans, to make one of our super sandwich spreads.

To 1 cup baked beans, add 1 to 2 tablespoons chopped dill pickle, 1 chopped tomato, 1 chopped hard-cooked egg, 1 dash cayenne, and 1 teaspoon grated onion. Add salt and freshly ground black pepper to taste. Combine thoroughly, spread on toasted whole wheat bread, and sprinkle with grated sharp Cheddar cheese. Run under a preheated broiler until the cheese is bubbling, then serve at once.

To 1 cup of baked beans, add ¼ cup chunky peanut butter, 2 tablespoons sweet pickle relish, and ¼ cup mayonnaise. Combine very well, spread on rye toast, and top with a small handful of alfalfa sprouts or watercress leaves.

Toast white or whole wheat bread and spread the slices with mayonnaise, then make the following layers: crisp lettuce, bubbling hot baked beans, sliced tomatoes, crisp bacon, thinly sliced Gruyère cheese. Broil the sandwiches until the cheese has melted and serve at once.

PINTO BEAN DIP

2 cups cooked
pinto beans,
drained

2 tablespoons
lard

1 teaspoon
minced garlic

1 teaspoon
bottled salsa
jalapeña

■ In a bowl with a fork or in a food processor, mash the beans to a coarse paste. Melt the lard in a heavy skillet over moderate heat, add the garlic, and sauté until it is golden. Stir in the beans and salsa, lower the heat, and simmer the beans for 5 minutes. Add salt to taste. Serve the dip hot with tortilla or corn chips.

• 2 CUPS

CHALUPAS JUAREZ

2 cups cooked pinto beans, drained and mashed

2 cups diced boneless roast pork

Salt

½ cup chopped canned mild green chilis, with juice

1 tablespoon minced garlic

1 teaspoon dried oregano

Freshly ground black pepper

1 cup corn or tortilla chips

1½ cups shredded iceberg lettuce

½ cup peeled, seeded, and chopped tomato

1½ cups grated Monterey Jack cheese

1 12-ounce jar red taco sauce

¼ cup finely chopped onion

■ In a mixing bowl combine the beans, pork, green chilis, garlic, and oregano. Salt and pepper to taste.

Arrange the corn chips on dinner plates. Over the chips arrange the following ingredients, mounding them decoratively: the bean-meat mixture, lettuce, tomato, onion, and finally the cheese. Serve with the taco sauce in a separate bowl.

• 8 to 10
SERVINGS

HUMMUS

2 cups cooked
garbanzos,
drained

¼ cup tahini

3 tablespoons
fresh lemon
juice

1 tablespoon
minced garlic

¼ teaspoon
ground cumin

Salt

Freshly
ground black
pepper

¼ cup chopped
parsley

• 10 to 12
SERVINGS

This famous Middle Eastern spread has by now become an American standard. It's great for parties, served alone or as one of a selection of hors d'oeuvres and accompanied by pita bread or crackers.

■ Place the garbanzos, tahini, lemon juice, garlic, and cumin, in a food processor. Salt and pepper to taste and blend until the mixture is a creamy purée, adding tablespoons of cold water if needed. Turn the hummus into a serving bowl or spread it out on a platter. Make decorative designs on the top with the tip of a knife and sprinkle with parsley.

WHITE BEAN DIP

2 tablespoons fruity olive oil

⅓ cup finely chopped green bell pepper

1 tablespoon minced garlic

⅓ cup finely chopped celery, including leaves

1½ cups cooked white beans, drained

½ teaspoon dried summer savory or oregano

½ teaspoon chili powder

½ teaspoon dried basil

¼ teaspoon ground coriander

1 teaspoon Dijon-style mustard

Freshly ground black pepper

½ cup plain lowfat yogurt

Salt

Great northern, navy, or cannelli beans are the base for this piquant dip that's perfect for crudités, miniature pita pockets, or crackers.

■ Heat the olive oil in a heavy skillet over moderate heat. Add the bell pepper, celery, and garlic, and sauté until the vegetables are barely soft. Scrape the vegetables into the bowl of a food processor fitted with a steel blade and add the beans, savory, chili powder, basil, coriander, mustard, vinegar, and yogurt. Process until the ingredients are puréed. Add salt and pepper to taste, and blend again. Turn into a serving bowl and chill before serving.

• About 2¼ CUPS

LIMA BEAN SPREAD

1 cup dried lima beans, picked over, rinsed, and soaked

1 stalk celery

3 sprigs fresh parsley

1 whole onion stuck with 2 whole cloves

½ bay leaf

½ teaspoon salt plus salt to taste

Heavy cream

2 tablespoons unsalted butter, cut into bits and softened

Freshly ground white pepper

■ Drain the beans, place them in a heavy saucepan with cold water to cover, and add the celery, parsley, onion, bay leaf, and salt. Cover and bring the mixture to a boil, reduce heat, and simmer gently for 3 hours, or until the beans are very tender, adding water as needed to keep the mixture very juicy and to provide 1 cup of cooking liquid to complete the recipe.

Drain the beans, reserving the 1 cup of the cooking liquid, and discard the vegetables. In a food processor, blend the beans, adding some of the cooking liquid and spoonfuls of cream to make a thick purée of spreading consistency. Stir in the butter and mix until it is incorporated. Season to taste with more salt and pepper. Cool and then chill before serving on toast or crackers.

• 2 CUPS

SOUTH OF THE BORDER DIP

2 cups cooked
Idaho red
beans or red
kidney beans,
puréed

1 tablespoon
unsalted butter
or margarine

4 ounces grated
Provolone or
Cheddar
cheese

4 bottled
jalapeño
peppers, finely
chopped

1 teaspoon
jalapeño
pepper juice

2 tablespoons
minced onion

1 clove garlic,
crushed

Serve this jalapeño dip over corn or tortilla chips or as a sauce for Red Bean Croquettes (page 32).

■ Place the puréed beans, butter, cheese, jalapeño peppers, pepper juice, onion, and garlic in the top of a double boiler, mix well, and cook over boiling water until the cheese is melted and the mixture is very hot.

• 2¼ CUPS

GARBANZO NUTS

1 **pound dried garbanzos (chickpeas), picked over, rinsed, and soaked**

2 **teaspoons salt plus salt to taste**

4 **ounces (1 stick) unsalted butter**

4 **cloves garlic, crushed**

½ **teaspoon dry mustard**

1 **teaspoon chili powder**

1 **teaspoon onion salt**

½ **teaspoon garlic salt**

People go nuts over these crunchy tidbits, which can be served with drinks before dinner or instead of croutons for soup. Freeze the garbanzo nuts on a baking sheet, transfer them to a plastic bag, and store in the freezer for up to three months. To serve, spread the frozen nuts out on a baking sheet and reheat under a preheated broiler for several minutes.

■ Drain the garbanzos, place them in a medium saucepan with cold water to cover, and bring to a boil over high heat. Lower the heat and simmer the beans until just tender, 1 to 1½ hours. Salt the beans lightly after 1 hour of cooking. Do not allow the garbanzos to become mushy. Drain the beans.

Over moderate heat, melt half the butter in each of 2 skillets. Add 2 garlic cloves to each skillet and sauté until the garlic is golden brown. Remove the garlic and add half the garbanzos to each skillet. Reduce the heat and sauté the beans very slowly, turning and stirring them often, until they begin to sizzle and become dark golden brown. When the garbanzos are crunchy on the outside and tender on the inside, they are done.

In a small bowl or cup mix the mustard, chili powder, 2 teaspoons salt, and onion salt. Sprinkle the mixture over 1 batch of garbanzos and toss lightly until thoroughly coated. In another bowl or cup, mix the garlic salt, ginger, and soy sauce and sprinkle over the second batch of garbanzos, tossing until the spice mixture and beans are well mixed. Turn each batch into a separate bowl and serve the garbanzos hot as soon as possible.

1 teaspoon powdered ginger

1 tablespoon soy sauce

• 2 to 3 CUPS

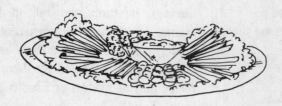

RED BEAN CROQUETTES

2 cups cooked
Idaho red beans
or red kidney
beans, drained
and mashed
while still hot

2 tablespoons
minced onion

½ teaspoon
dried oregano

1 can (4 ounces)
peeled green
chiles, drained
and chopped fine

¼ cup freshly
grated
Parmesan cheese

Salt

4 ounces sharp
Cheddar,
Provolone, or
Monterey Jack
cheese, cut
into 24 cubes

2 cups fine dry
bread crumbs

• 24 CROQUETTES

1 large egg beaten
with 1 tablespoon
water

Vegetable oil
for deep frying

These tasty morsels are delicious on their own or served with South of the Border Dip. Use them as cocktail nibbles for festive winter parties or as a side dish.

■ In a bowl, combine the mashed beans, onion, oregano, chiles, and Parmesan cheese and add salt to taste. Chill the mixture thoroughly. Shape the beans into 24 balls and insert a cube of cheese into the center of each. Roll the bean balls in the bread crumbs, dip into the egg mixture, and roll in bread crumbs again. Place the croquettes on a platter, cover with plastic wrap, and refrigerate until ready to fry them. The recipe may be made 4 or 5 hours ahead to this point.

Just before serving, in a deep heavy saucepan or a deep-fryer, heat 2 inches of the oil to 380°F. Add the croquettes, a few at a time, and fry until golden brown. Drain on paper towels. Serve hot, with cocktail picks if using as an hors d'oeuvre.

DILLED STRING BEANS

This is the simplest form of the classic recipe. The beans will taste and look their best if they are perfectly fresh and of uniform size.

■ Arrange the beans in a glass dish large enough to hold them or place them upright in 2 glass jars.

In a saucepan combine the water, vinegar, salt, dill, sugar, and red pepper flakes. Bring to a boil, and pour the mixture over the beans. Cover the dish or jars, cool the beans, and store in the refrigerator for at least 10 days before serving. Drain and serve chilled.

1 pound green beans, trimmed

1 cup water

¾ cup red or white wine vinegar

2 teaspoons salt

2 teaspoons dried dill weed

1 teaspoon sugar

¼ teaspoon red pepper flakes

• 3 CUPS

MAMA ROSSI'S

DILLY BEANS

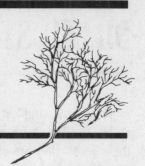

2 pounds green
  beans, trimmed

Salt

1 cup cooking
  liquid

1 clove garlic,
  split, plus 1
  whole garlic
  clove

¾ cup olive oil

½ cup red wine
  vinegar

Strained juice
  1 lemon

1 tablespoon
  snipped fresh
  dill

¼ teaspoon
  paprika

The Mediterranean-style dressing, used here with fresh beans, is equally effective as a marinade for cooked dried beans. It's best to make the beans from scratch, soaking them overnight before cooking, so they will absorb the dressing more readily.

■ Bring a large pot of water to a boil, add the beans and salt to taste, and cook the beans until they are just tender. Drain the beans and reserve 1 cup of the liquid. Cool the beans.

Rub a wooden salad bowl with the cut sides of the split garlic clove, then arrange the beans in the bowl. In a small bowl, combine the reserved cooking liquid, olive oil, vinegar, and lemon juice and pour the mixture over the beans. Add the dill, paprika, mint, and the whole clove of garlic and toss the mixture. Cover the bowl tightly with plastic wrap, and let stand at room temperature for 24 hours.

Place the beans upright in Mason-type jars and pour the liquid over them. Cover the jars and refrigerate the beans for at least 3 days. The longer they marinate, the better the flavor.

½ teaspoon
finely chopped
fresh mint

• 6 CUPS

COCONUT MILK

Fresh Coconut Milk

■ Place the coconut meat in a bowl, pour the hot water over it, and allow to sit for 30 minutes. Line a sieve with cheesecloth and strain the coconut milk into a bowl, squeezing the meat in the cheesecloth to extract all the liquid.

1 cup grated
fresh coconut
meat
2 cups hot water

Dried Coconut Milk

■ Follow the procedure above.

1 cup vacuum-
packed flaked
coconut
2 cups hot milk

• About 2 CUPS

GREEN BEANS IN COCONUT MILK

¼ cup olive oil

1 pound green beans, trimmed and split lengthwise

1 teaspoon salt

1 teaspoon sugar

1 bay leaf

1 cup coconut milk (recipe on page 35)

½ cup chopped onions

1 clove garlic

2 teaspoons grated lemon rind

• 4 to 6 SERVINGS

½ teaspoon dried ground chili peppers

1 large tomato, peeled, seeded, and chopped

■ Place the onions, garlic, lemon rind, chili powder, and tomato in a blender or food processor and process until the mixture forms a paste. Heat the oil in a heavy skillet over moderate heat, add the onion mixture, and sauté it, stirring constantly, for 3 minutes. Add the green beans, salt, sugar, bay leaf, and coconut milk, raise the heat, and bring to a boil. Cover the skillet, lower the heat, and simmer the beans for 20 minutes, or until very tender. Cool the beans and serve at room temperature.

SOUPS

PRESSURE COOKER
BAKED BEAN SOUP

2 cups
homemade
(pages 138
to 146) or
canned
baked beans

1½ cups canned
tomatoes,
with juice

1 onion, thinly
sliced

2 cups beef
bouillon

2 tablespoons
unsalted
butter,
softened

2 tablespoons
all-purpose
flour

• 4 to 5
SERVINGS

1 cup boiling
water

½ teaspoon
Worcestershire
sauce

Salt

Freshly
ground black
pepper

Croutons

■ In a 6-quart pressure cooker, combine the beans, tomatoes, onion, and beef bouillon. Seal the pressure cooker, bring it to 15 pounds of pressure, and process the soup for 5 minutes. Cool and open the cooker. Put the soup through a ricer or purée it in a food processor fitted with the steel blade, then pour it into a saucepan.

In a small bowl, cream the butter, work in the flour with a spoon, and stir in the boiling water. Blend well and add to the soup. Bring the soup to a boil, lower the heat, and simmer the soup slowly for about 5 minutes.

Add the Worcestershire sauce and season the soup to taste with salt and pepper. Serve in heated soup bowl with croutons.

CUBAN BLACK BEAN SOUP

2 cups dried black beans, picked over, rinsed, and soaked

2 quarts cold water

2 cups coarsely chopped celery

1 medium onion stuck with 4 whole cloves

8 ounces salt pork, cut into 1-inch cubes

1 teaspoon Worcestershire sauce

2 teaspoons fresh lemon juice

2 teaspoons salt

¼ teaspoon freshly ground black pepper

¼ cup dry sherry

6 thin slices lemon

■ Drain and rinse the beans. Place them in a soup kettle, add the celery, onion, and salt pork, and bring the mixture to a boil over high heat. Reduce the heat, and simmer the soup, covered, for about 3 hours, or until the beans are mushy. Remove the cloves from the onion and discard them.

In a food processor fitted with the steel blade, purée the soup in batches and return it to the kettle. Add the Worcestershire sauce, lemon juice, salt, and pepper and reheat until very hot and bubbling.

Just before serving, stir in the sherry. Serve in heated soup bowls and garnish with the lemon slices.

• 6 SERVINGS

GARBANZO AND SHRIMP SOUP

1½ cups cooked, drained garbanzos (chick-peas)

2 tablespoons vinegar

½ cup beer

5 cups beef bouillon

4 ounces shrimp, shelled, deveined, and coarsely chopped

½ cup grated turnip

1 cup grated carrot

4 large eggs

2 tablespoons soy sauce

½ cup chopped scallions, including green tops

• 6 to 8 SERVINGS

■ Purée the garbanzos in a food processor fitted with the steel blade or put them through a ricer. Scrape them into a bowl, add the vinegar and beer, and stir well. Let the mixture stand for 5 minutes.

Pour the bouillon into a medium saucepan and bring to a boil. Add the shrimp, turnip, and carrot, lower the heat, and simmer slowly for 1 minute. Add the bean mixture, stir well, and simmer 5 minutes longer.

In a small bowl, beat the eggs until light, add the soy sauce and scallions, and stir the mixture gently into the soup. Cook just until the eggs form strands. Serve the soup at once in heated soup bowls.

GAZPACHO ALICANTINA

1 quart chicken stock

2 tablespoons minced garlic

½ cup finely chopped red onion

1 small tomato, peeled, seeded, and cut into ½-inch dice

½ cup cooked garbanzos, well drained

½ small green bell pepper, seeded and cut into ½-inch dice

½ small cucumber, peeled, seeded, and cut into ½-inch dice

2 tablespoons fresh lemon juice

2 tablespoons fruity olive oil

2 tablespoons chopped pitted Calamata olives (optional)

Salt

Freshly ground black pepper

This hearty cold soup is like a liquid Mediterranean salad. It's sensational served for a summer luncheon accompanied by rounds of crusty French or Italian bread sprinkled with olive oil and Parmesan cheese and run under the broiler.

■ In a heavy saucepan, bring the stock to a simmer. Add the garlic, onion, tomato, cucumber, bell pepper, garbanzos, lemon juice, and olive oil and simmer the mixture, uncovered, for 3 minutes. Remove from the heat, cool the soup to room temperature, then chill. Add the olives, if desired, and salt and pepper to taste. Serve in chilled bowls.

• 4 to 6 SERVINGS

CURRIED SPINACH AND CHICK PEA SOUP

2 tablespoons clarified butter (recipe follows)

2 tablespoons minced garlic

1 bay leaf

1 quart cooked chick-peas, drained

2 cups chopped fresh spinach or ½ 10-ounce package frozen chopped spinach, thawed but not drained

6 cups meat, chicken, fish, or vegetable stock

1½ teaspoons curry powder

½ small zucchini cut into ¼-inch dice (about ½ cup)

¼ teaspoon ground dried thyme

¼ teaspoon ground cumin

2 tablespoons fresh lemon juice

½ cup grated carrot

¼ cup pearl barley

2 cups milk, scalded

Salt

Freshly ground black pepper

■ Heat the butter in a large, heavy saucepan over moderate heat. Add the garlic and sauté until it is golden. Add the stock, carrot, barley, and bay leaf and bring to a boil. Cover the pan, lower the heat, and simmer the mixture for about 1 hour, or until the barley is soft. Add the chick peas, spinach, zucchini, curry powder, thyme, and cumin. Return to a simmer and cook 3 minutes more. Add the lemon juice and simmer for 1 minute. Add the scalded milk and stir well; the milk will curdle slightly. Serve immediately in heated soup bowls.

• 8 to 10 SERVINGS

CLARIFIED BUTTER

Clarified butter is very useful for frying because less of it is needed than of ordinary butter, and it can be heated to higher temperatures.

8 ounces (2 sticks) unsalted butter

• About ¾ CUP

■ In a small, heavy saucepan, melt the butter over low heat, skimming the foam from the top from time to time. When the butter has melted, remove the pan from the heat and allow it to settle. Carefully pour the clear golden liquid into a bowl, leaving the sediment in the pan. Cool the clear butter, then chill. Clarified butter can be stored for months, tightly covered, in the freezer.

LENTIL AND BROWN RICE SOUP

½ cup lentils, picked over and rinsed

½ cup brown rice, well rinsed in warm running water

2 tablespoons olive oil

2 tablespoons minced garlic

¼ cup finely chopped onion

1 small carrot, cut into ¼-inch dice

½ stalk celery, cut into ¼-inch dice

1 large tomato, peeled, seeded, and cut into ¼-inch dice

3 to 4 cups veal or chicken stock or water

½ cup dry white wine

2 tablespoons soy sauce

1 large bay leaf

1 teaspoon dried basil

1 teaspoon paprika

1 teaspoon dried thyme leaves

Salt

Freshly ground black pepper

For a satisfying lunch or Sunday supper, serve this thick, rich soup with a cooked green vegetable or a leafy salad.

■ In a large, heavy saucepan, place the lentils, rice, oil, garlic, onion, carrots, celery, tomato, stock, wine, soy sauce, bay leaf, basil, paprika, and thyme. Salt and pepper to taste, place over high heat, and bring the mixture to a boil. Reduce the heat and simmer the soup, covered, for about 45 minutes, or until the rice and lentils are cooked but not mushy. Correct the seasonings and serve in heated soup bowls.

• **4 to 6 SERVINGS**

CURRIED LENTIL SOUP

½ cup lentils, picked over and rinsed

7 cups water

2 tablespoons unsalted butter

3 tablespoons finely chopped onion

1 clove garlic, finely chopped

¼ teaspoon dried ground chili peppers

2 teaspoons curry powder

1 teaspoon fresh lemon juice

1 teaspoon salt

■ Place the lentils and water in a large saucepan and bring to a boil over high heat. Reduce the heat and cook the lentils, covered, for about 1 hour, or until they are very tender.

In a small saucepan, melt the butter over low heat. Add the onions, garlic, chili peppers, and curry powder and sauté the mixture for 3 minutes, stirring constantly. Scrape the onion mixture into the lentils, stir in the lemon juice and salt, and continue cooking the soup for 15 minutes.

The soup can be served as is, or it can be puréed in a food mill, a food processor, or blender. Serve in heated soup bowls.

• **4 SERVINGS**

LENTIL CREOLE SOUP

4 ounces salt pork, cut into ⅛-inch dice

1 onion, finely chopped

1 stalk celery, finely chopped

½ cup finely chopped green bell pepper

½ cup finely chopped red bell pepper

1 teaspoon sugar

1 cup lentils

2 quarts water

1½ teaspoons salt

¼ teaspoon freshly ground black pepper

2 tablespoons catsup or tomato juice

2 tablespoons all-purpose flour

■ Place the salt pork in a large, heavy saucepan, place over moderate heat, and sauté until the pork has rendered its fat and is crisp. Drain the pork on paper towels and reserve.

Add the onion, celery, sugar, and bay leaf to the saucepan. Sauté until the vegetables have softened, about 5 minutes. Add the lentils, water, salt, and pepper to the pan and bring to a boil over high heat. Reduce the heat and simmer the soup, covered, for 1 hour, or until the lentils are very tender.

In a cup, mix the flour and catsup until well blended and stir in some of the hot soup. Pour the flour mixture into the soup, stir well, and add the green and red bell pepper. Cook the soup 5 minutes more and serve in heated soup bowls, garnished with the fried salt pork.

• 6 to 8 SERVINGS

LENTIL AND HAM SOUP

1 cup lentils, picked over and rinsed	1 Bermuda onion, finely chopped	1 quart beef broth
		Salt
2 cups water	1 carrot, finely chopped	Freshly ground black pepper
1 ham bone or end of ham, cut into pieces	2 tablespoons red wine vinegar	2 tablespoons chopped fresh parsley

■ In a large, heavy saucepan place the lentils, water, ham bone, carrot, and

47

vinegar. Bring to a boil over moderate heat. Reduce the heat and simmer the mixture, covered, until the lentils are very tender, about 1 hour.

Remove the ham bone from the soup, pick the meat from the bone, and cut it into small pieces. Reserve the ham. Purée the soup in a food processor fitted with the steel blade or force through a ricer or a food mill. Return the purée to the saucepan, add the broth, and season to taste with salt and pepper. Add the parsley and ham and bring the soup to a slow boil. Serve in heated soup bowls.

• 4 SERVINGS

RAZZLE DAZZLE LEMONY LENTIL SOUP

1½ cups lentils, picked over and rinsed

2 quarts rich chicken, veal, or vegetable stock

1 small unpeeled potato, cut into ½-inch dice

2 cups Swiss chard, cut into ½-inch dice

1 small onion cut into ½-inch dice

2 tablespoons minced garlic

½ cup chopped fresh parsley

■ Put the lentils into a large stockpot. add the stock, and bring to a boil over high heat. Lower the heat and simmer the lentils, covered, until they are very soft, about 45 to 50 minutes.

Add the potatoes to the soup and simmer, covered, for about 15 minutes, or until the potatoes are just cooked. Stir in the Swiss chard, onions, garlic, parsley, oil, lemon juice, and cumin. Simmer 2 minutes longer. Add the hot pepper sauce and season to taste with salt and pepper. Serve in heated soup bowls.

If the soup does not dazzle your tastebuds, add more hot sauce to your own soup and pass the bottle to your guests.

½ cup fruity olive oil

2 tablespoons fresh lemon juice

½ teaspoon ground cumin

2 teaspoons hot pepper sauce, or to taste

Salt

Freshly ground black pepper

• 6 to 8
SERVINGS

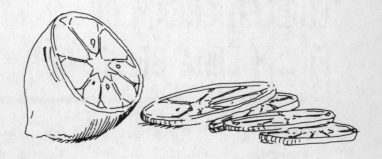

CUBAN LIMA BEAN SOUP

1 cup cooked fresh or dried lima beans, drained

½ cup blanched almonds

1 clove garlic

3 tablespoons vegetable oil

1 quart cold water

Salt

• 4 SERVINGS

Freshly ground black pepper

Sweet Hungarian paprika

2½ -inch slices sour dough bread, cut into 1½-inch squares

■ Remove and discard skins from lima beans. In a food processor fitted with the steel blade, grind the beans, almonds, and garlic to a paste. Scrape the bean paste into a heavy saucepan, add the oil, water, salt and pepper to taste, a light sprinkling of paprika, and the bread. Stir and bring just to a boil. Lower the heat and slowly simmer the soup, covered, for 30 minutes. Serve in heated soup bowls.

CHILLED CREAM OF FRESH LIMA BEAN SOUP

6 large leeks

6 cups shelled fresh lima

This elegant, subtle soup makes a splendid first course for a special summer party. Make the soup when fresh limas are available at your local markets or at farm stands and freeze it for later use. The soup tastes equally delicious hot.

■ Trim the leeks and discard the green parts. Wash the white parts thoroughly under running water and cut into 1-inch lengths. Place the leeks in a large soup kettle with the lima beans and chicken stock and bring the mixture to a boil over high heat. Lower the heat and simmer the soup, covered, for 30 minutes. Stir in the parsley, sauce diable, sugar, and nutmeg. Salt and pepper to taste. Cook a few minutes more to blend the flavors.

Purée the soup in a blender or food processor fitted with the steel blade. Transfer the mixture to a large bowl, cool, and chill well. Just before serving, stir in the cream and serve the soup in chilled bowls, garnished with the onion rings.

beans (about 3 pounds in shell)

3 quarts chicken stock

2 sprigs fresh parsley

1 tablespoon sauce diable

1 teaspoon sugar

½ teaspoon freshly grated nutmeg

Salt

Freshly ground white pepper

6 tablespoons heavy cream

1 red onion, thinly sliced and separated into rings

• 10 to 12
SERVINGS

CALIFORNIA-STYLE LIMA BEAN MINESTRONE

1 cup large dried lima beans, picked over, rinsed, and soaked

4 ounces salt pork, cut into ½-inch cubes

1 onion, finely chopped

1 clove garlic, finely chopped

6 cups water

2 beef or chicken bouillon cubes

1½ teaspoons salt

¼ teaspoon freshly ground black pepper

1 carrot, cut into ½-inch dice

1 turnip, cut into ½-inch dice

2 stalks celery, sliced

2 cups shredded cabbage

1½ cups canned tomatoes, with juice

½ bay leaf

¼ teaspoon dried basil

¼ cup rice

1 cup chopped raw spinach

½ cup freshly grated Parmesan cheese (optional)

■ Drain the beans. In a large, heavy saucepan sauté the salt pork over moderate heat until it releases some of its fat. Add the onion and garlic and sauté for 3 to 5 minutes, or until the onion is translucent. Add the drained lima beans, water, bouillon cubes, salt, and pepper and bring the mixture to a boil. Add the carrot, turnip, celery, cabbage, tomatoes, and bay leaf, reduce the heat, and simmer the soup, covered, for 1½ hours.

Add the rice and basil and cook 30 minutes longer, or until the rice is tender and all the flavors have blended. Stir in the spinach during the last 10 minutes of cooking and taste the soup for seasoning. Serve in heated soup bowls, sprinkled with the cheese, if desired, and accompanied by toasted rounds of French or Italian bread.

• 8 SERVINGS

BEST-EVER LIMA

BEAN SOUP

1 cup large dried lima beans, picked over, rinsed, and soaked

1 meaty ham bone

1 quart water

1 onion, quartered

4 leafy celery tops

8 slices lemon

4 whole cloves

1 teaspoon dry mustard

1 teaspoon salt

¼ teaspoon freshly ground black pepper

1 cup milk

Croutons

■ Drain the beans and place them in a large saucepan, add the ham bone, water, onion, celery tops, 2 slices of lemon, the cloves, the mustard, salt, and pepper. Bring to a boil, reduce the heat, and cook the soup, covered, for

1½ to 2 hours, or until the lima beans are tender, adding water if necessary to keep the soup from getting too thick.

Remove the ham bone, lemon slices, and cloves. Strip the meat from the ham bone, cut it into small pieces, and reserve. Purée the bean mixture in a blender or food processor fitted with a steel blade. Return the purée to the saucepan, add the ham and milk and heat almost to the boil. Taste for seasoning and serve in heated soup bowls with the croutons.

• 4 SERVINGS

UNITED STATES SENATE RESTAURANT BEAN SOUP

2 pounds dried navy beans, picked over, rinsed, and soaked

4 quarts hot water

1½ pounds

smoked ham hocks

2 tablespoons unsalted butter

1 onion, chopped

Salt

Freshly ground black pepper

■ Drain and rinse the beans and put them in a large soup kettle with the 4 quarts of water and the ham hocks.

Bring to a boil, reduce heat, and simmer the soup, covered, for about 3 hours, adding more water as necessary.

In a skillet, melt the butter over moderate heat, add the onion, and sauté until translucent, about 5 minutes. Add the onions to the soup with salt and pepper to taste. Serve in heated soup bowls.

• **10 to 12 SERVINGS**

BUTTER BEAN AND HAM CHOWDER

1½ cups dried butter beans (lima beans), picked over, rinsed, and soaked

1 quart water

1 meaty ham hock

1½ teaspoons salt

¼ teaspoon freshly ground black pepper

2 tablespoons unsalted butter

1 cup finely chopped onion

½ cup finely chopped green bell pepper

1½ cups canned cream-style corn

1 quart milk, scalded

■ Drain the beans and place them in a large soup kettle. Add the ham hock and bring the mixture to a boil over high heat. Reduce the heat and simmer the soup, covered, for about 1½ hours, or until the beans are tender. Add the salt and pepper 30 minutes before the beans have finished cooking.

Drain the beans, reserving 1 cup of cooking liquid. Remove and discard the skin and bones from the ham hock and shred the meat. Mash 1 cup of the lima beans.

In the kettle, melt the butter over moderate heat, add the onion and green pepper, and sauté them until the onion is translucent, 3 to 5 minutes. Stir in the corn, the mashed and whole lima beans, reserved cooking liquid, ham, and scalded milk. Heat until very hot, but do not allow to boil. Serve at once in heated soup bowls.

• 4 to 6
SERVINGS

BASIC BEAN AND HAM SOUP

This and the two soups that follow are quintessential peasant fare. In any of the recipes you can omit the ham bone and vinegar and use water or vegetable stock as the liquid, for a delicious meatless potage. Other vegetables and herbs and spices can be added to change the soup to suit your palate and your menu. Long, slow cooking of all the ingredients, as in this soup and Navy Bean Soup Alameda, will result in a complete blending of all the flavors. For greater textural contrast, but equally savory effect, try Navy Bean and Ham Soup.

Depending on the occasion, you might wish to purée the soup and even to add half-and-half or heavy cream for a touch of elegance. The amount of liquid in this recipe will yield a fairly thick soup. If you want a lighter dish, simply add more liquid at the beginning and check often to see that the soup is at a constant level.

■ Drain and rinse the beans, lentils, or split peas and put them into a large soup

2 cups dried beans, lentils, or split peas, picked over, rinsed and soaked (lentils and split peas need not be soaked)

2 quarts water or beef, veal, or chicken stock

1 meaty ham bone

2 onions, coarsely chopped

2 cloves garlic, minced

2 carrots, sliced or cut into ¼-inch dice

2 stalks celery, sliced

(*cont.*)

57

1 bay leaf

2 tablespoons vinegar

Salt

Freshly ground black pepper

• 6 to 8 SERVINGS

kettle with the water, ham bone, onions, garlic, carrots, celery, bay leaf, and vinegar and bring to a boil over high heat. Reduce the heat, cover, and simmer the soup until the beans are tender, adding liquid as needed. If you intend to puree the soup, cook the beans until they are somewhat mushy.

Remove the ham bone. pick off the meat, shred and reserve it. Discard the bone. Remove the bay leaf. Purée the soup, if desired, in a foc¹ processor or a food mill. Add the reserved ham, season with salt and pepper to taste, and serve in heated soup bowls.

NAVY BEAN SOUP ALAMEDA

1 cup dried navy beans, picked over, rinsed, and soaked

1 quart water

1 ham bone, split

½ cup chopped onion

2 stalks celery, chopped

2 tablespoons minced green bell pepper

2 medium carrots, chopped

½ cup tomato purée

⅛ teaspoon mustard

1 tablespoon vinegar

1 whole clove

2 black peppercorns

Salt

Freshly ground black pepper

Chopped parsley

■ Drain and rinse the beans and put them into a large soup kettle with the water, ham bone, carrots, celery, green pepper, tomato purée, mustard, vinegar, clove, and peppercorns. Bring to a boil, lower the heat, and simmer the soup, covered, 4 hours, stirring often and adding more water as needed.

Remove the ham bone, scrape off and chop any meat on the bone, and add to the soup. Add salt and pepper to taste. Serve in heated soup bowls sprinkled with chopped parsley.

• 4 to 6
SERVINGS

NAVY BEAN AND HAM SOUP

8 ounces smoked ham, cut into 1-inch cubes

6 cups water

1 cup dried navy beans, picked over, rinsed, and soaked

1 carrot, thickly sliced

2 turnips, thickly sliced

1½ cups thinly sliced onion

2 medium potatoes, peeled and cut into ½-inch dice

1 cup tomato sauce

2 teaspoons salt

Freshly ground black pepper

5 tablespoons chopped fresh basil or parsley

■ Place the ham and water in a soup kettle, bring to a boil, lower the heat, and simmer, covered, for 1 hour. Drain and rinse the beans, add to the kettle, and simmer, covered, for about 2 hours, or until the beans are tender, adding more water as necessary. Add the carrot, turnips, onion, potatoes, and tomato sauce. Salt and pepper to taste and cook, covered, until the vegetables are tender, 20 to 30 minutes. Serve in heated soup bowls garnished with the basil.

• 8 SERVINGS

ORIENTAL NAVY BEAN AND PUMPKIN SOUP

2 tablespoons unsalted butter

1 cup diced (¼-inch) zucchini

1 cup diced (¼-inch)

mushrooms (see note below)

1 large bay leaf

½ teaspoon freshly grated nutmeg

The original recipe for this delicious soup called for fresh, pine-scented, wild Matsutaki mushrooms, which, alas, are only very rarely available. Fortunately, fresh or dried and soaked Shiitake mushrooms are much easier to find, and they make an admirable substitute.

■ In a heavy saucepan, melt the butter over moderate heat, add the zucchini, mushrooms, bay leaf, and nutmeg. Sauté for 5 minutes, or until the vegetables are tender. Stir in the bean and pumpkin purées and the stock and bring the soup to a simmer. Add salt and pepper to taste and serve in heated soup bowls.

2 cups cooked navy beans, drained and puréed

2 cups unsweetened pumpkin purée

2 cups rich chicken stock

Salt

Freshly ground white pepper

• 4 to 6
SERVINGS

NAVY BEAN, BEER, AND CHEESE SOUP

4 tablespoons (½ stick) unsalted butter

¼ cup all-purpose flour

1 quart chicken stock

¼ cup finely chopped celery

¼ cup finely chopped carrots

2 tablespoons finely chopped green bell pepper

1 cup cooked navy beans,

drained and puréed

⅛ teaspoon freshly ground white pepper

Salt

1 cup beer

¼ cup freshly grated Parmesan cheese

Garlic-flavored croutons

Paprika

• 4 to 6 SERVINGS

■ In a heavy saucepan melt the butter over moderately low heat, stir in the flour and cook, stirring constantly, for 2 to 3 minutes, without allowing the roux to brown. Gradually stir in the broth, raise the heat to moderate, and cook until the sauce is thickened, stirring constantly. Add the celery, carrot, and bell pepper and simmer, covered, until the vegetables are tender, about 15 minutes. Add the beans and stir until the mixture is well blended. Season with the pepper and salt to taste and stir in the beer and cheese. Serve in heated soup bowls sprinkled with the croutons and a dash of paprika.

WHITE BEAN AND SPINACH SOUP

2 beef bouillon cubes	1 tablespoon all-purpose flour blended with 2 tablespoons cold water	Salt
3 cups cooked chopped spinach		Freshly ground black pepper
		1 cup dried white beans, picked over, rinsed, and soaked

■ Drain the beans and place in a soup kettle with the water. In a skillet, melt the butter over moderate heat, add the onion and garlic, and sauté until the onion is soft. Add the onion and garlic to the kettle with the bay leaf and bring to a boil over high heat. Reduce the heat and cook the soup, covered, for about 2 hours, or until the beans are very tender.

Add the water, bouillon cubes, and spinach to the soup and bring to the boiling point. Slowly stir in the flour mixture. Season to taste with salt and pepper and simmer the soup for 5 minutes. Serve in hot soup bowls.

2 quarts beef stock or water

1 bay leaf

1 onion, finely chopped

1 clove garlic, gently crushed

2 tablespoons unsalted butter

2 cups water

• 8 to 10 SERVINGS

MINESTRONE

¼ cup fruity olive oil

¾ cup chopped onion

1 tablespoon minced garlic

1 cup chopped celery, including tops

1 cup diced potatoes

1 cup shredded cabbage

1 cup diced green beans

1 cup fresh or canned coarsely chopped plum tomatoes

6 cups beef or chicken broth or water

2 cups cooked cannellini or navy beans, drained

1 cup cooked macaroni or other small pasta

Salt

Freshly grated black pepper

½ cup freshly grated Parmesan cheese

¼ cup chopped fresh parsley

There are countless versions of minestrone—Italian vegetable soup. This recipe, which hails originally from southern Italy, can be varied in as many ways as you like, depending on the season and your own inclination. Turnips, zucchini, fresh fava beans, and rice are good additions or substitutions. Long, slow cooking of minestrone ensures the best result. The soup tastes even better the next day served hot or at room temperature dusted with strips of fresh basil leaves.

■ In a large, heavy kettle heat the olive oil over moderate heat. Add the onion and garlic and sauté for 3 minutes, or until the onion begins to turn yellow. Add the celery, potatoes, cabbage, and green beans and sauté for 6 to 8 minutes more. Add the tomatoes and broth and bring to a boil. Reduce the heat and simmer the soup, covered, for about 3 hours, adding broth or water as needed to keep the vegetables from sticking to the bottom of the kettle. The minestrone should be very thick.

Stir in the cooked beans, and the pasta. Salt and pepper to taste and cook 15 minutes longer. Add the Parmesan and stir well. Serve in heated soup bowls sprinkled with the parsley.

• **6 to 8 SERVINGS**

WHITE BEAN SOUP AND DUMPLINGS

1 cup dried white beans, picked over, rinsed, and soaked

2 quarts beef stock

2 carrots, sliced

1 parsnip, sliced

2 ounces (½ stick) unsalted butter

2 onions, finely chopped

1¼ cups sifted all-purpose flour

2 teaspoons salt

½ teaspoon freshly ground black pepper

1 teaspoon paprika

1 large egg

2 tablespoons water

3 frankfurters, sliced

■ Drain and rinse the beans and put them into a soup kettle. Add the stock, carrots, and parsnips and bring to a boil over high heat. Reduce the heat and simmer the soup, covered, for 2 hours. In a blender or food processor purée 1 cup of the beans, then stir the purée into the kettle.

In a skillet melt the butter over moderate heat. Add the onions and sauté them until brown, stirring often. Sprinkle 2 tablespoons of the flour over the onions and cook, stirring, until the flour has been absorbed. Gradually stir in 1 cup of the soup and cook, stirring constantly, until the liquid is thickened. Scrape the onion mixture into the kettle, add salt, pepper, and paprika, and simmer the soup, covered, for 1 hour.

To make the dumplings, sift the remaining flour into a bowl. Make a well in the center and add the egg and water and mix in the flour until a pastelike dough is formed. Knead the dough on a lightly floured surface for about 6 to 8 minutes, or until it no longer sticks to the fingers. On a lightly floured surface, roll out the dough very thin and let rest, uncovered, for 45 minutes. Pinch off walnut-size pieces of the dough and drop into the boiling soup. Cook the dumplings until they float.

Fry the frankfurter slices for 5 minutes, drain, and add to the soup. Serve at once in heated soup bowls.

• 6 SERVINGS

PINTO BEAN CHILI SOUP

2 cups dried pinto beans, picked over, rinsed, and soaked

2 quarts water

Beef, veal, or chicken stock

1 teaspoon salt

1 teaspoon sugar

¼ teaspoon freshly ground black pepper

¼ teaspoon dried thyme leaves

¼ teaspoon dried sage

1½ teaspoons chili powder dissolved in 1 tablespoon cold water

1 tablespoon unsalted

butter, softened

1 tablespoon all-purpose flour

■ Drain and rinse the beans and put them in a soup kettle with the water. Bring the water to a boil, lower the heat, and cook the beans, covered, for 2 hours, or until they are tender.

With a slotted spoon remove 2 cups of the beans from the pot and reserve them. Purée the remaining beans and their liquid in a food processor. Measure the purée and add an equal amount of beef, veal, ham, or chicken stock, or use water and bouillon cubes. Pour the purée and stock into the kettle and add the salt, sugar, pepper, thyme, sage, and chili powder mixture. Bring the soup to a simmer and cook slowly, covered, for 25 minutes.

Cream the butter and flour in a small bowl. Stir in ½ cup of the hot soup and pour the mixture into the soup. Bring the soup to a boil, add the reserved beans, and simmer for 5 minutes. Serve in heated soup bowls.

• 4 to 6
SERVINGS

BEST RED BEAN SOUP

2 cups dried Idaho red beans or kidney beans, picked over, rinsed, and soaked

2 quarts water

1 meaty ham bone

2 onions, quartered

2 carrots, cut into 2-inch pieces

2 stalks celery, cut into 2-inch slices

Bouquet garni: 3 sprigs fresh parsley, 3 whole cloves, and 2 small bay leaves tied in a cheesecloth bag

1 teaspoon dry mustard

¼ teaspoon dried thyme leaves

1 dash ground mace

2 tablespoons balsamic or red wine vinegar

2 teaspoons Worcestershire sauce

Salt

Freshly ground black pepper

¼ cup sherry or Madeira

½ cup sour cream

2 hard-cooked eggs, finely chopped

1 lemon or lime, thinly sliced

■ Drain and rinse the beans and return to the kettle with the 2 quarts of water, the ham bone, onions, carrots, celery, bouquet garni, mustard, thyme, mace, vinegar, and Worcestershire sauce. Bring the soup to a boil, lower the heat, and simmer, covered, for 3½ to 4 hours, or until the beans are very soft. Stir occasionally while cooking and add hot water as necessary to keep the beans from sticking to the bottom of the kettle.

Remove the ham bone and cut the meat into small pieces. Reserve the ham. Skim any fat from the surface of the soup, then purée the beans and vegetables in a food processor or food mill. Return the soup to the kettle. If the purée is too thick, add hot water until the soup is the consistency you want. Add the ham and salt and pepper to taste. Reheat the soup over moderately low heat, stirring often to keep it from scorching.

Just before serving, stir in the wine. Serve the soup in a heated tureen or individual heated soup bowls with the sour cream swirled across the surface and the chopped eggs sprinkled on top. Float the lemon slices on the soup and serve at once.

• 4 to 6
SERVINGS

SPLIT PEA AND SAUSAGE SOUP

1 cup green
split peas

3 quarts water

1½ cups coarsely
chopped
onions

½ cup diced
carrot

¼ cup chopped
celery, with
leaves

2 large bay
leaves

3 tablespoons
chopped
fresh parsley

1 pinch
cayenne
pepper

1 pound lean
sausage
meat

Salt

Freshly ground
black pepper

1 cup toasted
rye bread
croutons

This is pea soup with a difference. Instead of cooking the split peas with a ham bone, which flavors the entire soup, this recipe calls for simmering peas and aromatic vegetables in water (or stock, if you want a richer soup) until just tender enough to purée. Right before serving, crisp, browned sausage meat is stirred into the soup, offering a tasty contrast in textures and flavors. This is a real crowd pleaser.

■ Wash and drain the peas. Put them into a large, heavy soup kettle with the water, onions, carrot, celery, parsley, bay leaves, and cayenne pepper. Bring to a boil, lower the heat, and cook for 45 minutes to 1 hour, or until all the ingredients are very soft.

Remove the bay leaves and purée the peas and vegetables in a food processor, blender, or food mill. Return the purée to the stock pot.

Place the sausage meat in a heavy skillet, place over moderately low heat, and cook the meat, breaking up the lumps with a wooden spoon, until the meat has rendered its fat and is browned. Drain the sausage meat on paper towel and stir into the soup.

Reheat the soup, add salt and pepper to taste, and serve in heated soup bowls garnished with the croutons.

• **10 to 12 SERVINGS**

WASHINGTON STATE FISHERMEN'S SPLIT PEA SOUP

1 3- to 4- pound beef tongue

1 large onion

This is the traditional soup eaten by the fishermen of Puget Sound.

■ Wash the beef tongue well. Place it in a large enameled or stainless steel kettle with the onion, celery, carrot, clove, bay leaf, and thyme. Add cold water to cover the ingredients, measuring the water before you pour it in, then add ¾ to 1 teaspoon of salt for every quart of water. Cover the kettle and bring the water to a boil, lower the heat, and simmer the tongue for 3 to 4 hours, or until a fork inserted into the thickest part comes out easily.

Remove the tongue from the kettle. Strain and measure the stock, then add enough water to make 2 quarts. Pour the stock and water into the kettle, add the peas, and bring to a boil. Lower the heat, cover the kettle, and simmer the peas until they are soft, about 35 to 40 minutes.

While the peas are cooking, peel the tongue, cutting away any small bones and gristle, and cut 2 or 3 ¼-inch slices for each serving. Wrap the slices in foil and keep them warm. Reserve any remaining tongue for another recipe.

Add the half-and-half to the soup and return to a simmer. Add more salt, if needed, and pepper to taste. Place the tongue slices in wide, heated soup bowls, pour the soup over the tongue, and serve at once.

1 stalk celery, with leaves

1 large carrot

1 whole clove

1 bay leaf

¼ teaspoon dried thyme

Salt

2 cups dried green split peas

2 cups half-and-half

Freshly ground black pepper

• 6 to 8 SERVINGS

PURÉE MONGOLE

4 ounces (1 stick) unsalted butter or margarine

¼ cup chopped onion

¼ cup chopped carrot

¼ cup chopped celery

¼ cup chopped green bell pepper

½ cup diced unpeeled red apple

1 cup diced cooked boneless chicken

2 teaspoons curry powder

⅓ cup all-purpose flour

Although Purée Mongole originated in India, versions of it have appeared in American cookbooks since the late nineteenth century. The recipes that follow are very different from each other in seasonings and character. What they do have in common, however, are two ingredients: peas and tomatoes. And of course, they are both very tasty. If your guests have never eaten Purée Mongole before, prepare them for a delicious and unusual combination of flavors.

■ Melt the butter in a large, heavy saucepan over moderate heat. Add the onion, carrot, celery, green pepper, apple, and chicken and sauté until the vegetables are soft. Stir in the curry powder and sauté for 2 to 3 minutes more. Add the flour and cook, stirring constantly, for about 3 minutes. Stir in the tomato purée, nutmeg, cloves, and parsley and cook, stirring constantly, until the mixture is very thick. Stir in the chicken stock and cook until the soup reaches a simmer. Add the rice and peas and return the soup to a simmer. Cook, stirring occasionally, for 5 minutes. Add salt and pepper to taste.

Purée the soup in a food mill or food processor and reheat before serving in heated soup bowls.

1 cup tomato purée

¼ teaspoon nutmeg

1 pinch ground cloves

2 tablespoons chopped parsley

5 cups chicken stock

2 cups hot cooked rice

2 cups hot cooked split peas, drained

Salt

Freshly ground black pepper

• 6 to 8 SERVINGS

HENRI CHARPENTIER'S PURÉE MONGOLE

4 ounces fresh
green beans,
trimmed and
cut into 1-inch
pieces

4 ounces
shelled fresh
lima beans

4 ounces
shelled fresh
peas

1 cup cooked
navy beans,
drained and
rinsed

½ stalk celery,
coarsely
chopped

This is a wonderful soup to make for luncheon in mid-summer, when fresh green beans, limas, peas, and tomatoes are all at their peak.

■ In a heavy saucepan, place the green beans, limas, peas, navy beans, celery, and onion, add water to cover, and bring to a boil over high heat. Lower the heat and cook the vegetables, covered, until they are very tender, 40 to 50 minutes, adding water as necessary to keep them from sticking to the bottom of the pan.

While the vegetables are cooking, put the tomatoes into a heavy saucepan, season to taste with salt and pepper, and bring to a boil over high heat. Lower the heat and simmer the tomatoes, covered, for about 20 minutes, or until they have become a thick purée.

When the vegetables are tender, drain off the liquid reserving some of it. Purée the vegetable mixture in a food processor, adding some of the reserved liquid to make a thick purée. Return the vegetable purée to the saucepan, add the milk and consommé, and bring to a boil. Add the tomatoes and simmer the soup, covered, for 20 minutes to blend the flavors.

Place the cream and butter in the bottom of a heated soup tureen and pour in the simmering soup, stirring well. Taste again for seasonings and serve in heated soup bowls.

1 medium Bermuda onion, coarsely chopped

5 tomatoes, peeled, seeded, and coarsely chopped

2 cups milk

1 quart beef or chicken consommé

Salt

Freshly ground black pepper

½ cup heavy cream

1 tablespoon unsalted butter

• 6 to 8 SERVINGS

STRING BEAN SOUP

1 tablespoon
olive oil

1 clove garlic,
gently crushed

1 tablespoon
tomato sauce
mixed with ¾
cup water or 2
tomatoes,
peeled,
seeded, and
chopped

4 ounces young
green beans,
trimmed and
cut into 1-inch
pieces

Salt

Freshly ground
black pepper

4 slices toast

■ In a heavy, medium saucepan, heat the oil over moderate heat, add the garlic and brown lightly. Remove the garlic and discard. Add the diluted tomato sauce or fresh tomatoes to the pan. Lower the heat and, if you are using fresh tomatoes, cook them at a simmer for 20 minutes. Add the green beans and season them to taste with salt and pepper. Cover the saucepan and simmer the beans until they are tender, about 10 to 12 minutes, adding a little hot water occasionally to keep the beans from sticking and the consistency thick.

Place a slice of toast in each heated soup bowl and pour the soup over it. Serve at once.

• 4 SERVINGS

CREAM OF GREEN BEAN AND ASPARAGUS SOUP

1 cup fresh or
frozen green
beans, cut into
1-inch pieces

1 cup fresh or
frozen
asparagus, cut
into 1-inch
pieces

½ cup diced
unpeeled potato

½ cup chopped
onion

1 large bay leaf

1 teaspoon
dried basil

1 tablespoon
snipped fresh
dill or 1
teaspoon
dried dill

3 cups chicken
stock

2 tablespoons
unsalted
butter

2 tablespoons
all-purpose
flour

1 cup milk,
scalded

Salt

Freshly
ground white
pepper

Freshly grated
nutmeg

6 sprigs fresh
dill or 2
tablespoons
chopped fresh
parsley

■ Place the green beans, asparagus, potato, onion, bay leaf, basil, and dill weed in a large saucepan with the chicken stock and bring to a boil over high heat. Reduce the heat and simmer the soup, covered, until the vegetables are tender.

In a small saucepan melt the butter over moderately low heat and stir in the flour. Cook, stirring constantly with a

wooden spoon for 2 to 3 minutes, but do not allow the roux to brown. Off heat, add the milk all at once, stirring constantly, and return the sauce to the heat. Cook, stirring constantly, for 3 minutes or until the sauce is thick and smooth.

Add the cream sauce to the soup, stirring constantly, until all the ingredients are blended. Add salt, pepper, and nutmeg to taste. Serve in heated soup bowls garnished with a sprig of dill or chopped parsley.

• **4 to 6 SERVINGS**

VEGETABLE CHOWDER

1 cup green beans, cut into 1-inch lengths	1 cup diced cauliflower	1 tablespoon sugar
	3 small new potatoes, peeled and quartered	Salt
1½ cups shelled fresh or frozen lima beans		2 cups water
		1 cup chopped spinach
2 carrots, thinly sliced	4 radishes, trimmed and halved lengthwise	3 tablespoons unsalted butter
		1 tablespoon all-purpose flour

■ In a large kettle, place the green beans, limas, carrots, cauliflower, potatoes, radishes, and sugar. Salt to taste and add the water. Bring to a boil over high heat, reduce the heat, and simmer the vegetables, covered, until tender, about 30 to 40 minutes. Add the spinach and cook 5 to 7 minutes longer.

Melt the butter in a large soup kettle over moderately low heat, stir in the flour, and cook, stirring constantly, for 2 to 3 minutes. Add the hot milk, stirring constantly, until the mixture is smooth. In a bowl, beat together the egg yolk and cream. Beat in a ladleful of the hot milk mixture, stirring constantly, then pour the yolk mixture into the milk, stirring until the mixture is blended. Add the vegetables with their liquid and the shrimp and heat the soup thoroughly, but do not allow to boil. Serve in heated soup bowls sprinkled with parsley.

2 quarts hot milk

1 egg yolk

7 tablespoons light cream or half-and-half

1 cup coarsely chopped cooked shrimp

Chopped fresh parsley

• 8 SERVINGS

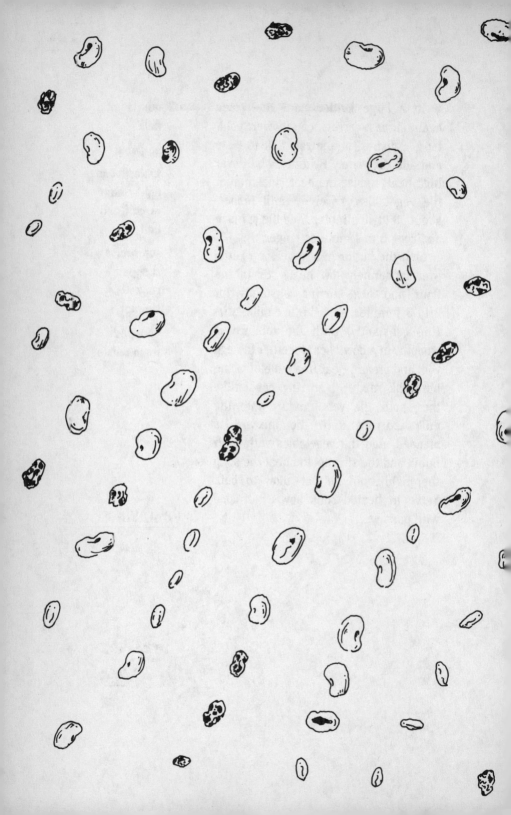

SALADS

BAKED BEAN

SALAD LORENZO

1 cup baked
beans,
homemade
(page 142) or
canned

1 cup
sauerkraut,
squeezed dry
and coarsely
chopped

1 tablespoon
finely
chopped
green olives

1 tablespoon
finely
chopped
sweet pickles

½ cup olive oil

¼ cup red wine
vinegar

½ cup bottled
chili sauce

½ cup finely
chopped
watercress
leaves

Salt

Freshly
ground black
pepper

Lettuce leaves

■ In a mixing bowl combine the beans, sauerkraut, olives, and pickles. In a small bowl blend until smooth the oil, vinegar, chili sauce, and watercress. Salt and pepper to taste. Pour the dressing over the bean mixture, toss lightly, and chill.

Arrange lettuce leaves on chilled salad plates and divide the salad among the plates.

• 4 SERVINGS

BEAUTIFUL BAKED BEAN SALADS

Cold leftover baked beans are very good in themselves, and thrifty cooks have long known that they taste even better mixed with other vegetables and then dressed with a piquant vinaigrette. Each of the following salads can either be made with cold ingredients and served at once, or mixed beforehand and then chilled. These recipes are for 4 servings, but they can easily be doubled or tripled for larger gatherings.

■ Mix 1 cup of baked beans with 1 cup chopped or sliced unpeeled apple. Toss in ¼ cup chopped toasted walnuts, almonds, or pecans and dress with a mustard vinaigrette.

■ Mix 1 cup baked beans with ½ cup peeled, seeded, and diced cucumber, ½ cup peeled and diced tender raw turnip, and ¼ cup diced radishes or celery. Sprinkle with 2 tablespoons each chopped parsley and toasted sesame seeds. Toss with vinaigrette.

■ Mix 1 cup baked beans with ½ cup diced beets, 2 chopped hard-cooked eggs, and 2 tablespoons chopped pickles or pickle relish. Toss lightly with vinaigrette.

BARBECUE BEANS SALAD

1 can (1 pound) barbecue beans

½ cup finely chopped celery

2 tablespoons finely chopped green bell pepper

• 4 to 6 SERVINGS

1 tablespoon finely chopped onion

Salt

Freshly ground pepper

1 head lettuce, torn into bite-size pieces

■ In a bowl combine the beans, celery, bell pepper, and onion. Salt and pepper to taste, cover, and chill.

Distribute the lettuce on chilled salad plates and arrange the bean salad on top.

KIDNEY BEAN SALAD

2 cups canned
   kidney beans,
   drained and
   rinsed

4 slices crisp
   cooked bacon,
   crumbled

⅓ cup finely
   chopped
   onion

½ cup finely
   chopped
   celery

1 cup diced
   unpeeled
   apple

⅓ cup diced
   Cheddar
   cheese

½ teaspoon salt

Freshly
   ground black
   pepper

Mayonnaise

■ In a mixing bowl, combine the beans, bacon, onion, celery, apple, and cheese. Salt and pepper to taste. Add just enough mayonnaise to moisten. Toss gently and chill.

• 4 SERVINGS

CHILI-SPICED RED

BEAN SALAD

2 cups canned
red kidney
beans,
drained and
rinsed

2 cups canned
whole kernel
corn, drained

½ cup diced
celery

½ cup sliced
scallions,
including
green tops

2 tablespoons
chopped
parsley

¼ cup finely
chopped
bottled chilis

Salt

Freshly ground
black pepper

¾ cup olive oil

¼ cup red wine
vinegar

1 teaspoon
minced garlic

1 teaspoon chili
powder

1 teaspoon
dried
marjoram

1 teaspoon
ground cumin

■ In a large bowl, combine the beans, corn, celery, scallions, parsley, and chilis. Salt and pepper to taste. In a small bowl blend together the oil, vinegar, garlic, chili powder, marjoram, and cumin. Pour the dressing over the bean mixture, toss well, and taste for seasonings. Chill the salad and serve on cold plates.

• 6 to 8
SERVINGS

KIDNEY BEAN AND HORSERADISH SALAD

Horseradish is a wonderful comple-ment to the beans, mayonnaise, and sour cream. For those who like a more pronounced horseradish flavor, pass a small bowl of it at the table. This salad tastes equally delicious made with gar-banzos, pinto, or cranberry beans.

■ In a mixing bowl combine the beans, celery, and onion. In a small bowl blend well the mayonnaise, sour cream, and horseradish. Salt and pepper to taste. Fold the dressing into the bean mixture and chill the salad. Serve nestled in let-tuce cups.

1 quart canned red kidney beans, drained and rinsed

½ cup chopped celery

¼ cup finely chopped onion

¼ cup mayonnaise

¼ cup sour cream

2 teaspoons white horseradish

Salt

Freshly ground black pepper

Lettuce

• 4 SERVINGS

RED BEAN AND

RICE SALAD

½ cup long-grain
or converted
rice

2 cups canned
kidney beans,
drained and
rinsed

1 cup finely
sliced celery

1 medium green
bell pepper,
finely
chopped

1 tablespoon
minced onion

1 hard-cooked
egg, chopped

2 tablespoons
lowfat yogurt

1 tablespoon
finely
chopped
parsley

1 teaspoon
dried basil

½ teaspoon
dried mint

Salt

Freshly ground
pepper

Yogurt and chopped fresh herbs
make a refreshing dressing for this
extra-healthy salad.

■ Cook the rice according to package
instructions, making sure that the rice
does not overcook and that each grain
is separate. Turn the cooked rice into a
mixing bowl, add the beans, green pepper, celery, onion, and egg, and mix
gently. In a small bowl, blend well the
yogurt, parsley, basil, and mint. Salt and
pepper to taste. Fold the dressing into
the salad, toss lightly, and chill.

• 6 SERVINGS

MOLDED KIDNEY BEAN SALAD

2 cups cooked kidney beans, drained

2 hard-cooked eggs, finely chopped

1 teaspoon grated onion

½ cup finely chopped celery

½ cup finely chopped dill pickle

½ cup mayonnaise, preferably homemade (page 104)

¼ teaspoon salt

2 tablespoons fresh lemon juice

2 tablespoons water

1 envelope unflavored gelatin

1 cup warmed evaporated milk

■ In a mixing bowl combine the beans, eggs, onion, celery, pickle, mayonnaise, and salt and mix well.

In a custard or measuring cup, combine the lemon juice and water. Sprinkle the gelatin over the top and let stand 5 minutes to soften. Place the cup in a saucepan containing 1 inch of simmering water and stir gelatin until it is dissolved. Remove the cup from the pan and stir the gelatin into the warm evaporated milk.

Pour the gelatin mixture into the beans, stir carefully to distribute it evenly, and ladle the salad into an oiled 5-cup ring mold. Cover with plastic wrap and chill the salad until set, about 4 hours.

Unmold the salad over a platter lined with lettuce leaves. Garnish with raw seasonal vegetables.

• 8 SERVINGS

KIDNEY BEAN AND SAUSAGE SALAD

½ cup long-grain or converted rice

8 ounces bulk sausage meat

2 cups cooked red kidney beans, drained and rinsed

1 medium Bermuda onion, finely chopped

½ cup thinly sliced celery

1 green bell pepper, thinly sliced

3 sweet pickles, coarsely chopped

1 tomato, peeled, seeded, and cut into ¼-inch dice

1 hard-cooked egg, coarsely chopped

2 tablespoons finely chopped parsley

¼ cup olive oil

¼ cup red wine vinegar

1 clove garlic, gently crushed

1 pinch dried oregano

Salt

Freshly ground black pepper

Crisp greens

■ Cook the rice according to package instructions, taking care that each cooked grain is separate. Turn the rice into a mixing bowl.

In a heavy skillet over moderate heat, cook the sausage until lightly browned, breaking up the meat with a wooden spoon. Add the sausage to the rice and stir. Add the beans, onion, celery, green pepper, pickles, tomato, egg, and parsley. Stir gently to mix.

In a small bowl, blend the oil, vinegar, garlic, and oregano. Salt and pepper to taste. Let stand for about 30 minutes, then remove and discard the garlic. Pour the dressing over the salad and toss well. Chill the salad and serve over greens.

• 6 SERVINGS

SWEET AND

SOUR RED BEANS

5 cups cooked red beans or kidney beans, drained

⅔ cup thinly sliced celery

⅔ cup coarsely chopped Bermuda onion

⅔ cup sugar

1 teaspoon salt

½ teaspoon coarsely ground black pepper

½ cup vegetable oil

⅔ cup cider or garlic-flavored wine vinegar

■ Place beans, celery, and onion in a mixing bowl. In a small bowl, combine the sugar, salt, pepper, oil, and vinegar. Pour the dressing over the vegetables and mix lightly. Cover and chill for 24 hours. Serve very cold.

• 6 to 8 SERVINGS

PICKLED RED BEANS, IDAHO STYLE

2 cups dried
Idaho red
beans or
kidney beans,
picked over,
rinsed, and
soaked

6 cups water

2 tablespoons
unsalted
butter or
vegetable oil

1 medium onion

1 cup coarsely
chopped
Spanish onion

1 cup vegetable
oil

¼ cup red wine
vinegar

½ teaspoon dry
mustard

2 teaspoons salt

½ teaspoon
coarsely
ground black
pepper

½ teaspoon
sugar

1 clove garlic,
pierced with a
wooden
toothpick

■ Drain and rinse the beans and place
them in a kettle over high heat with the
water, butter, and whole onion, and
bring to a boil. Reduce the heat and
simmer the beans, covered, for about 2
hours, or until they are tender, adding
water from time to time to keep the
beans from scorching. Drain the beans
and discard the onion.

Place the warm beans in a mixing
bowl and add the chopped onion. In a
small bowl, combine well the oil, vinegar, mustard, salt, pepper, and sugar.
Pour the dressing over the beans and
onions and toss together lightly. Bury
the garlic clove in the beans. Allow the

salad to cool to room temperature, then cover the bowl with plastic wrap and refrigerate the salad for at least 2 days and up to a week to allow the flavors to blend and mellow.

• 4 to 6
SERVINGS

THREE-BEAN SALAD

1 cup green beans, cut into 1-inch lengths, cooked until crisp-tender and still warm

2 cups cooked great northern beans, drained and still warm

2 cups cooked Idaho red or kidney beans, drained and still warm

½ cup olive oil

½ cup red wine vinegar

2 cloves garlic, gently crushed

¼ teaspoon dried oregano, crushed

Salt

Freshly ground black pepper to taste

1 large Spanish onion, thinly sliced and separated into rings

½ cup thinly sliced celery

½ cup diced sharp Cheddar cheese

Fresh green beans and Cheddar cheese spark this unusual version of a classic American salad. If you're feeling more traditional, use equal amounts of great northerns, red beans, and garbanzos and omit the cheese. This salad will taste even better if all the beans are

dressed as soon as they've been cooked
—that way they'll absorb more of the
vinaigrette. Serve on a bed of greens
with hot garlic bread for a light and perfectly balanced luncheon or supper.

■ Place the green, great northern, and
red beans in separate bowls.

In a small bowl, combine well the oil,
vinegar, garlic, and oregano. Salt and
pepper to taste. Pour about one-quarter
of the dressing over the green beans
and divide the remaining dressing between the other 2 bowls. Toss to mix.
Cover each bowl and refrigerate the
beans overnight.

Turn all the beans into a large chilled
bowl. Add the onion rings, celery, and
• 6 SERVINGS cheese and toss lightly.

SIMPLE LENTIL SALAD

Simple and simply delicious, this versatile salad can be varied to suit the mood of the meal by the addition of fresh herbs and any number of diced raw or blanched vegetables. Red and green vegetables will look especially pretty. Experiment by using different proportions of oil and vinegar in the vinaigrette. For a curried lentil salad, add 1 teaspoon of curry powder, heated in a dry skillet until the curry aroma is released. Or you can try a yogurt dressing —don't use too much or it will overwhelm the delicate flavor of the lentils —spiced with ground cumin, then garnish the salad with chopped fresh mint. Be sure to cook the lentils just until they are tender but still firm.

2 cups cooked lentils, still warm

1 clove garlic, minced

¼ cup olive oil

¼ cup vinegar

½ teaspoon paprika

Salt

Freshly ground black pepper

1 tablespoon finely chopped parsley

■ Place the lentils in a mixing bowl. In a small bowl, combine the garlic, oil, vinegar, and paprika. Salt and pepper to taste. Pour the dressing over the lentils and mix gently.

Serve the salad still slightly warm, at room temperature, or chilled.

• 6 SERVINGS

LENTIL AND ANCHOVY SALAD

2 cups cooked
lentils, drained
and cooled

1 tablespoon
drained capers

1 tablespoon
finely chopped
dill pickle

1 tablespoon
chopped
parsley

1 tablespoon
snipped chives

3 tablespoons
olive oil

1 tablespoon
tarragon
vinegar

3 anchovy fillets,
drained and
chopped

Freshly ground
black pepper

Greens

■ In a mixing bowl, combine the lentils, capers, pickle, parsley, and chives. In a small bowl, blend well the oil, vinegar, anchovies, and pepper to taste. Pour the dressing over the salad, mix gently but thoroughly, and chill. Serve on a bed of greens.

• 4 SERVINGS

GREEN BEAN AND PARMESAN SALAD

■ Place beans in a mixing bowl. In another bowl, combine well the onion, oil, and vinegar. Salt and pepper to taste. Add the Parmesan, stir until well mixed, and pour over the beans. Toss the salad and chill, if you want to serve it cold. (Note that the beans will discolor if they stand for too long in the vinaigrette.)

Serve the salad chilled or at room temperature over a bed of crisp greens.

1 pound cold cooked green beans, cut into 2-inch lengths

1 small onion, finely chopped

½ cup olive oil

¼ cup wine vinegar

Salt

Freshly ground black pepper

½ cup freshly grated Parmesan cheese

Romaine leaves

• 4 to 6
SERVINGS

GREEN BEAN
SALAD NIÇOISE

2 cups cold cooked green beans, cut into 1-inch lengths

2 cups cold diced cooked potatoes

2 medium tomatoes, quartered

4 anchovy fillets, drained and finely chopped

4 brine-cured black olives, pitted and thinly sliced

1 tablespoon drained capers

1 tablespoon chopped fresh basil

6 tablespoons olive oil

2 tablespoons fresh lemon juice

Freshly ground black pepper

1 small head Boston lettuce, the leaves separated, washed, and patted dry

• 4 SERVINGS

Our version of this famous Provençal salad is made without tuna fish, which makes it the perfect appetizer or salad course for a light supper.

■ In a mixing bowl combine the green beans and potatoes. Add the tomatoes, anchovies, olives, capers and basil and toss gently. In a small bowl mix well the oil, lemon juice, and pepper to taste.

In a salad bowl, toss the lettuce leaves with 3 tablespoons of dressing. Pour the remaining dressing over the green bean mixture and toss lightly. Arrange the beans over the lettuce and serve at once.

POTATO AND GREEN BEAN SALAD

1 pound small new potatoes

1 pound green beans, trimmed

1 cup thinly sliced red onion rings

1 cup thinly sliced green bell pepper rings

½ cup diced celery

¼ cup chopped parsley

¼ cup vegetable or olive oil

¼ cup red wine vinegar

¼ teaspoon dried oregano

Salt

Freshly ground black pepper

■ Place the potatoes in a medium saucepan, cover generously with cold water, add a pinch of salt, and bring to a boil over high heat. Continue boiling until the potatoes are three-quarters done, about 15 minutes. Add the green beans and boil until both beans and potatoes are just cooked. Drain the vegetables and cool to room temperature.

Cut the potatoes into 1-inch dice, leaving their skins on, and place in a bowl. Cut the green bean into 1-inch lengths and add to the potatoes. Add the onion rings, green pepper, celery, and parsley. In a small bowl, combine well the oil, vinegar, and oregano. Salt and pepper to taste. Pour the dressing over the vegetables and toss gently but well. Serve at room temperature.

• 6 to 8 SERVINGS

CABBAGE AND GREEN BEAN SLAW

2 cups shredded cabbage

1½ cups green beans, trimmed

¼ cup finely chopped Bermuda onion

¼ cup finely chopped celery

2 tablespoons shredded red bell pepper or bottled pimiento cut into fine julienne

Mayonnaise

This crunchy salad is especially good served with pork, duck, or game. Be sure all the ingredients are cold before they are mixed. Best Foods™ mayonnaise (called Hellman's™ east of the Rockies) is the dressing of choice.

■ Place the cabbage, green beans, onion, celery, and red pepper in a mixing bowl and toss. Distribute the slaw among salad plates and serve with a separate bowl of mayonnaise.

• 4 to 6 SERVINGS

WAX BEAN AND TRUFFLE SALAD

Nothing could be simpler to make than this wildly extravagant salad, consisting only of wax beans, homemade mayonnaise subtly flavored with fresh savory, and truffles. Do not attempt it unless the beans are young, tender, and just plucked from the vine.

■ In a saucepan, cook the beans and savory in lightly salted water to cover for about 10 minutes, or until the beans are crisp-tender. Do not overcook. Drain the beans, place in a mixing bowl, and cool to room temperature.

Add the mayonnaise to the beans, toss gently, and chill. Arrange lettuce leaves on individual salad plates, mound the beans over the lettuce, and sprinkle with the chopped truffles.

3 pounds yellow wax beans, trimmed and cut into ½-inch lengths

2 teaspoons finely chopped fresh savory

Salt

1 cup homemade mayonnaise (page 104) mixed with 1 teaspoon finely chopped savory

3 fresh or canned black truffles, finely chopped

Lettuce leaves

• 6 to 8 SERVINGS

HOMEMADE MAYONNAISE

1 egg yolk

½ teaspoon Dijon-style mustard

¼ teaspoon salt

2 teaspoons fresh lemon juice, or to taste

½ cup corn or peanut oil mixed with ½ cup olive oil

• About 1 CUP

■ Place the egg yolk, mustard, salt, and lemon juice in a blender container and blend until the ingredients are well mixed. With the motor running, add ¼ cup of the oil mixture a drop at a time. When the mayonnaise begins to emulsify, add the remaining oil in a thin stream. Taste the mayonnaise and correct the seasonings, adding lemon juice or hot water by the teaspoonful to thin the mixture, if necessary. Scrape the mayonnaise into a jar, cover tightly, and refrigerate for up to 3 days.

CURRIED LIMA BEAN AND SPINACH SALAD

2 tablespoons
butter

1 small onion,
finely chopped

1 clove garlic,
finely chopped

1 teaspoon curry
powder

1 cup dried lima
beans, picked
over, rinsed,
and soaked

1 cup beef
bouillon

1 cup dry white
wine

8 ounces spinach,
stems removed,
washed, patted
dry, and chilled

2 tablespoons
olive oil

1 tablespoon
white wine
vinegar

Salt

Freshly ground
black pepper

• 4 SERVINGS

■ In a heavy saucepan, melt the butter over medium heat. Add the onion and garlic and sauté for 2 to 3 minutes. Add the curry powder and cook, stirring for 2 to 3 minutes more. Drain the beans and add them to the pan with the bouillon, white wine, and enough water to cover the beans. Bring to a boil, lower the heat, and simmer the beans, covered, until they are tender, about 1 hour. Do not allow the beans to become mushy. Drain the limas, place them in a large salad bowl, and allow to cool.

Add the spinach to the salad bowl. In a small bowl, mix the oil and vinegar. Salt and pepper to taste, and pour the dressing over the salad. Toss gently and taste for seasoning.

HAM AND LIMA BEAN SALAD

1 cup cooked fresh lima beans

1 cup cooked cold ham or beef, cut into thin strips

½ cup diced unpeeled apple

½ cup cooked diced carrot

Salt

Freshly ground black pepper

2 tablespoons sour cream

¼ cup heavy cream, whipped

Juice ½ lemon

Be sure all the ingredients are cold before you begin to assemble this salad.

■ In a salad bowl combine the beans, ham, apple, and carrot. Salt and pepper to taste.

In a small bowl thoroughly blend the sour cream, whipped cream, and lemon juice. Lightly fold the dressing into the salad and serve at once.

• 4 SERVINGS

PIQUANT LIMA BEAN SALAD

3 cups cooked large dried lima beans, drained and cooled

1 green bell pepper, coarsely chopped

½ cup sliced scallions, including green tops

1 cup thinly sliced celery

½ cup sour cream

1½ teaspoons caraway seeds

½ cup finely chopped dill pickles

1 teaspoon salt

1 tablespoon salad oil

1 tablespoon prepared horseradish

Salad greens

■ In a mixing bowl place the lima beans, green pepper, scallions, and celery. In a small bowl, combine the sour cream, caraway seeds, pickles, salt, oil and horseradish. Fold the dressing into the bean mixture and chill slightly.

Line a serving bowl with the salad greens and mound the lima salad over them.

• 6 to 8 SERVINGS

CHUCK-WAGON

LIMA BEAN SALAD

1 clove garlic,
  split
1 cup cooked
  large dried
  lima beans,
  drained and
  chilled
2 stalks celery,
  thinly sliced
½ unpeeled
  cucumber,
  thinly sliced
2 medium
  tomatoes, cut
  into wedges
2 hard-cooked
  eggs, coarsely
  chopped

1 quart torn
  crisp salad
  greens
¼ cup salad oil
2 tablespoons
  red wine
  vinegar

½ cup crumbled
  blue cheese
Salt
Freshly
  ground black
  pepper

■ Rub a salad bowl with the cut sides of the garlic and discard the garlic. Place the lima beans, celery, cucumber, tomatoes, eggs, and salad greens in the bowl and toss lightly.

In a small bowl, combine well the oil, vinegar, and blue cheese. Salt and pepper to taste. Pour over the salad and toss gently. Serve on chilled plates.

• 4 SERVINGS

BEAN AND BARLEY PILAF SALAD

1½ cups cooked navy or other white beans, drained

4 ounces green beans, cooked until crisp-tender and cut into ½-inch pieces

¾ cup cooked pearl barley, drained

½ cup peeled, seeded, and diced cucumber

¼ cup finely chopped pitted black olives, preferably Greek or Italian

¼ cup chopped scallions

½ cup lowfat plain yogurt

2 tablespoons tahini

¼ cup olive oil

¼ cup red wine vinegar

2 teaspoons finely chopped fresh basil or ½ teaspoon dried

2 teaspoons chopped fresh marjoram or ½ teaspoon dried

2 teaspoons snipped fresh dill or ½ teaspoon dried

Salt

Freshly ground black pepper

Salad greens

This recipe can be doubled or tripled and used to great advantage for a buffet party.

■ In a mixing bowl, combine the navy beans, green beans, barley, cucumber, olives, and scallions and mix lightly. In a small bowl, blend well the yogurt, tahini, oil, vinegar, basil, marjoram, and dill. Salt and pepper to taste. Pour the dressing over the vegetables and mix gently but well. Cover the salad with plastic wrap and refrigerate for at least 1 hour to allow the flavors to blend.

Arrange salad greens on individual serving plates or on a platter, mound the salad over them, and serve at once.

‹ 4 to 6
SERVINGS

NAVY BEAN

SALAD COLORADO

1 clove garlic, split

1 cup cooked dried white or navy beans, drained and cooled

2 small beets, cooked, peeled, and sliced

8 ounces green beans, cooked until crisp-tender and cut into 1-inch lengths

1 cup finely chopped celery

4 scallions, thinly sliced

¼ cup finely chopped green bell pepper

1 bunch watercress, tough stems discarded

3 hard-cooked egg yolks

110

■ Rub a salad bowl with the cut sides of the garlic and discard the garlic. Add to the bowl the navy beans, green beans, beets, celery, green pepper, scallions, and watercress.

In a blender container, place the egg yolks, mustard, oil, and vinegar. Salt to taste, add a generous grinding of pepper, and blend until the dressing is smooth. Pour over the salad and toss lightly. Serve on chilled salad plates.

1 teaspoon tarragon or Dijon-style mustard

5 tablespoons olive oil

2 tablespoons red wine vinegar

Salt

Freshly ground black pepper

• 4 SERVINGS

CHICKEN AND GARBANZO BEAN SALAD

3 cups diced cooked chicken

2 cups cooked garbanzos, drained

6 medium tomatoes, cut into ½-inch dice

3 green bell peppers, chopped

½ cup mayonnaise, preferably homemade (page 104)

Salt

Freshly ground black pepper

Crisp salad greens

(cont.)

3 hard-cooked
   eggs,
   quartered

6 radishes

6 ripe olives

• 6 SERVINGS

This main course salad should be served as soon as it's assembled, so be sure all the ingredients are cold before you prepare it.

■ In a large mixing bowl, combine the chicken, beans, tomatoes, green peppers, and mayonnaise. Salt and pepper to taste. Toss gently but thoroughly.

Arrange the salad greens on a serving plate, mound the salad in the center, and garnish with the eggs, radishes, and olives.

TEN-VEGETABLE POTPOURRI

2 cups canned garbanzo beans, drained and rinsed

2 cups canned red kidney beans, drained and rinsed

2 cups canned wax beans, drained

1 cup canned green beans, drained

1 cup canned whole-kernel corn, drained

1 cup canned lima beans, drained and rinsed

1 cup canned diced carrots, drained

½ cup thinly sliced raw mushrooms

½ cup diced cooked crookneck squash or zucchini

½ cup finely chopped green bell pepper

Here's our version of that American favorite, the church supper many-bean salad—easy to fix and perfect for a crowd.

■ In a large mixing bowl, place the garbanzos, kidney beans, wax and green beans, corn, lima beans, carrots, mushrooms, squash, and green pepper. In a small bowl, mix well the oil, vinegar, sugar, garlic powder, hot pepper sauce, and Parmesan. Salt and pepper to taste. Use a light hand with the salt, because canned vegetables tend to be quite salty. Pour the dressing over the vegetables and toss well. Cover the bowl with plastic wrap and refrigerate until the salad is well chilled.

1 cup olive oil

½ cup red wine vinegar

¼ cup light brown sugar

¼ teaspoon garlic powder

1 teaspoon hot pepper sauce

½ cup freshly grated Parmesan cheese

Salt

Freshly ground white pepper

• 12 to 15 SERVINGS

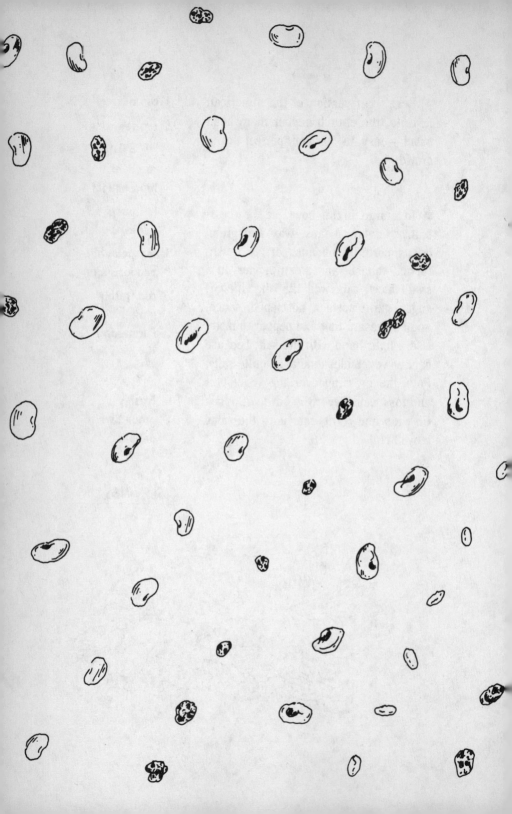

SIDE DISHES

PURÉED BLACK BEANS
WITH SOUR CREAM

2 cups dried
black beans,
picked over,
rinsed, and
soaked

6 cups water

½ cup olive oil

1 large onion,
finely chopped

2 cloves garlic,
minced

1 green bell
pepper, finely
chopped

1 bay leaf

1 teaspoon salt

½ teaspoon
freshly ground
black pepper

3 tablespoons red
wine vinegar

Delicious served with roast pork or chicken.

■ Drain and rinse the beans and place them in a large heavy kettle with the water. In a skillet, heat the oil over moderate heat, add the onion, garlic, and green pepper, and sauté until the vegetables are wilted and the onion is translucent, about 5 minutes. Add the vegetables to the beans and bring the mixture to a boil. Reduce the heat, cover the kettle, and cook the beans until they are tender, 1½ to 2 hours, adding water as necessary to keep the mixture moist.

Add the salt, pepper, and vinegar and purée the beans in a food processor. Return the mixture to the kettle and reheat gently. Turn the beans into a serving bowl or spread on a platter. Sprinkle with the parsley and serve with the onion rings arranged on top of the beans or serve the onion rings separately. Pass a bowl of sour cream.

• 4 to 6
SERVINGS

2 tablespoons chopped parsley

2 medium red onions, thinly sliced and separated into rings

Sour cream

CUBAN-STYLE MOORS AND CHRISTIANS

1½ cups black beans, picked over, rinsed, and soaked

4 slices lean bacon, chopped fine

½ clove garlic, gently crushed

1 onion, finely chopped

2 tablespoons mango chutney

1 teaspoon chili powder

Salt

Cayenne

Beef, veal, or chicken stock

2 cups hot fluffy boiled or steamed rice

In this spicy dish, black beans (Moors) are cooked to a thick rich sauce for the Christians—fluffy white grains of rice.

■ Drain the beans, cover with fresh water, and bring to a boil over high heat. Reduce the heat and simmer the beans, covered, until just tender, 1½ to 2 hours.

While the beans are cooking, in a skillet, fry the bacon until crisp and drain it on paper towels. Drain the beans and return them to the kettle. Add the bacon, garlic, onion, chutney, and chili powder. Add salt and cayenne pepper to taste, and pour in enough stock to cover the beans. Stir the mixture well and bring to a boil over moderate heat. Reduce the heat and simmer the sauce, covered, until the beans begin to disintegrate and the sauce thickens.

Mound the rice in a deep heated serving dish and spoon the sauce over it. Serve at once.

• 4 to 6
SERVINGS

SAUTÉED WHOLE WHEAT BERRIES, BARLEY, AND BLACK-EYED PEAS

⅓ cup whole wheat berries (available in health food stores)

1½ cups water

½ cup pearl barley

¼ cup vegetable oil

½ cup finely chopped onion

¼ cup finely diced (¼-inch) carrots

1 teaspoon chopped fresh oregano or ¼ teaspoon dried oregano

1 teaspoon chopped fresh coriander (cilantro; optional)

Salt

Freshly ground black pepper

⅓ cup chopped parsley

1 cup cooked black-eyed peas, drained

1 tablespoon fresh lemon juice

1 teaspoon chopped fresh dill or ¼ teaspoon dried dill

1 teaspoon chopped fresh basil or ¼ teaspoon dried basil

A wonderful, crunchy combination, this dish can be served as an accompaniment to spicy meat and chicken main courses or, mounded on such greens as arugula, watercress, or romaine, as a hot salad course.

■ In a small, heavy saucepan bring the whole wheat berries and water to a boil over moderate heat. Lower the heat, cover the pan, and cook the berries until they are tender but not mushy, about 35 to 40 minutes—the berries should still have some crunch. Drain the whole wheat berries and reserve.

Cook the barley, following package instructions. Drain and set aside.

In a heavy skillet, heat the oil over moderate heat, add the onion and carrots, and sauté until the carrots are crisp-tender. Stir in the reserved whole wheat berries and barley, the black-eyed peas, lemon juice, dill, basil, oregano, and coriander. Salt and pepper to taste. Sauté, stirring gently, until the mixture is blended well and heated through. Taste for seasoning and serve sprinkled with the parsley.

• 6 to 8
SERVINGS

REFRIED BEANS

We offer here the most basic form of this old Mexican standby. Embellish this recipe as your fancy moves you, beginning with the beans themselves, which can be cooked with onions and garlic—sautéed or not—and flavored with cumin, bay leaves, or epazote, a Mexican herb. Then, the fried, puréed beans might be refried with more sautéed onions and garlic. However you choose to make them, refried beans are a satisfying dish served with a topping of sour cream or grated Cheddar or Monterey Jack cheese (perhaps melted under the broiler). The beans are used as one of the staple components in Mexican tortilla dishes and as an accompaniment to spicy Mexican sausages.

1 pound dried pink or red beans, picked over, rinsed, and soaked

2 quarts water

Salt

1 cup less 2 tablespoons bacon drippings, lard, or vegetable oil

■ Drain and rinse the beans and place them in a large kettle, add the water, and bring to a boil over high heat. Lower the heat and cook the beans, covered, until they are tender and mushy, 1½ to 2 hours. As the beans cook, add enough water to keep them from sticking to the

kettle; the juices should be thick. Add salt to taste.

Coarsely purée the beans in batches in a food processor with the steel blade. Add ½ cup of the fat to a heavy skillet and place over high heat. When the fat is very hot, add the bean purée and cook, stirring, until the beans are dry and have absorbed the fat. Cool the beans.

To refry the beans, heat 2 table-spoons of oil in a skillet until hot, add the fried beans, and cook, stirring constantly, until the beans have absorbed the oil. Continue adding the remaining oil, 1 or 2 tablespoons at a time, stirring the beans constantly to keep them from sticking, until they are very hot and creamy in texture.

• 6 SERVINGS

OLD SOUTHERN HOPPING JOHN

In this version of the classic, the rice is cooked along with the cow peas. However, if you prefer the flavors to be blended only at the last minute, cook the rice separately in lightly salted water and add it to the tender, drained cow peas when it is tender and fluffy.

■ Place the beans in a large, heavy saucepan, add the water and smoked meat, and bring to a boil over high heat. Reduce the heat, and simmer the cowpeas until they are barely tender, about 25 to 30 minutes.

Ladle out all but 3 cups of the cooking liquid, add the rice, and simmer the mixture until the rice is tender and all the liquid is absorbed, about 35 to 40 minutes for brown rice and about 18 minutes for white rice. Season with salt and pepper to taste. Serve very hot.

2 cups fresh cow peas

2 quarts water

4 ¼ -inch- thick slices smoked salt pork or smoked bacon, cut in half

1 cup brown or white rice

Salt

Freshly ground black pepper

• 6 SERVINGS

CRANBERRY
BEAN SUCCOTASH

1 pound dried cranberry beans, picked over, rinsed, and soaked

1 can (46 ounces) tomato juice

2 tablespoons unsalted butter

1 package (10 ounces) frozen green beans, thawed

1 package (10 ounces) frozen corn kernels, thawed

1 onion, finely chopped

1 clove garlic, finely chopped

1 green bell pepper, finely chopped

2 medium tomatoes, coarsely chopped

2 tablespoons chopped parsley

Salt

Freshly ground black pepper

½ cup freshly grated Parmesan cheese

Cranberry beans are an interesting substitute for limas, one of the traditional succotash ingredients. This recipe serves twelve happy people and can be prepared and assembled ahead of time except for the final baking.

■ Drain the beans and place in a large kettle with the tomato juice and butter and bring to a boil over high heat. Lower the heat and simmer the beans, covered for 2½ to 3 hours, or until they are tender.

Preheat the oven to 350°F. Butter a 3-quart casserole and into it put the cranberry beans, green beans, corn, onion, garlic, green pepper, tomatoes, parsley, and salt and pepper to taste. Mix well. Sprinkle the top of the mixture with the Parmesan and bake, uncovered, for 30 minutes, or until the cheese is delicately browned.

• **12 SERVINGS**

GARBANZO BEANS IN TOMATO SAUCE

1 pound dried garbanzos, picked over, rinsed, and soaked

1½ quarts water

2 cloves garlic, finely chopped

1 large onion, finely chopped

⅓ cup olive oil

2 cups canned Italian plum tomatoes, with juices

1 jar pimientos, cut into thick strips

Salt

Freshly ground black pepper

■ Drain the beans, put them into a large kettle with the water, garlic, onion, and oil, and bring to a boil. Reduce the heat, cover the kettle, and simmer the garbanzos for 1 hour. Add the tomatoes and continue cooking the beans until they are tender and the liquid has reduced. During the last 15 minutes of cooking, add the pimientos and season to taste with salt and pepper.

• **4 to 6 SERVINGS**

GARBANZO BEANS

WESTERN STYLE

1 can (1 pound) garbanzos, drained and rinsed

½ cup coarsely chopped black olives

½ cup finely chopped celery

1 tablespoon finely chopped Bermuda onion

½ cup catsup

1 tablespoon red wine vinegar

1 tablespoon Worcestershire sauce

Salt

Freshly ground black pepper

■ Preheat the oven to 400°F. Grease a 1-quart casserole. In a mixing bowl, combine the garbanzos, olives, celery, onion, catsup, vinegar, Worcestershire and sauce. Salt and pepper to taste. Mix thoroughly, turn into the casserole, and bake for 20 minutes, or until bubbly.

• 4 SERVINGS

FARMER'S LIMA BEANS

4 slices lean bacon, finely chopped

1 tablespoon all-purpose flour

1 cup chicken broth

2 pounds fresh lima beans, shelled

1 teaspoon grated orange rind

⅛ teaspoon freshly ground white pepper

¼ cup heavy cream

1 tablespoon chopped parsley

Salt

■ In a skillet over moderate heat, sauté the bacon until it is transparent and has released most of its fat. Pour off all but 1½ tablespoons of the fat, sprinkle the flour over the fat remaining in the skillet, and stir well with a wooden spoon until the mixture is well blended. Gradually add the broth and cook, stirring constantly, until the sauce is slightly thickened. Add the beans, orange rind, and pepper, cover the pan, and reduce the heat to very low. Simmer the beans for 30 minutes, or until they are tender, stirring occasionally. Add the cream and parsley. Salt to taste and stir well. Serve hot.

• 4 to 6 SERVINGS

127

CANDIED NAVY BEANS

1½ cups dried navy or pea beans, picked over, rinsed, and soaked

2 canned pimientos, finely chopped

2 medium apples, unpeeled, cored and diced

Salt

Freshly ground black pepper

2 tablespoons chopped walnuts or pecans

1 tablespoon brown sugar or honey

1 tablespoon unsalted butter or bacon drippings

• 4 to 6 SERVINGS

■ Drain the beans and place in a large saucepan, add cold water to cover the beans by 1 inch. Bring to a boil over high heat, lower heat, and simmer beans, covered, for 1½ to 2 hours, or until tender.

Preheat the oven to 400°F. Grease a 1½-quart casserole. Drain the beans and return to the saucepan. Add the pimientos, and apples. Salt and pepper to taste and mix well. Turn the mixture into the casserole, sprinkle with the sugar and nuts, and bake, uncovered, until hot and bubbly.

CAJUN-STYLE RED BEANS

This recipe calls for 2 teaspoons of red pepper sauce, but because we have never figured out how to take the hot out of the pot, we suggest that you add it slowly, tasting as you go, and then pass the bottle for your guests to add for themselves.

■ In a skillet over medium heat, brown the sausage meat, breaking it up with a wooden spoon. Drain the sausage.

Drain the beans and place them in a large kettle with the sausage meat, ham bone, onions, garlic, green pepper, bay leaves and cumin. Cover with cold water and bring to a boil over high heat. Lower the heat and simmer the mixture, covered, for 1 to 1½ hours, or until the beans are tender but not mushy.

Remove the ham bone, strip off the meat, and cut it into small pieces. Return the ham to the pan. Stir in salt to taste, then slowly add the hot pepper sauce, tasting the beans as you go.

½ **pound bulk pork sausage**

1 **pound kidney beans, picked over, rinsed, and soaked**

1 **meaty ham bone, cracked twice**

1½ **cups coarsely chopped onions**

2 **tablespoons minced garlic**

¼ **cup diced green bell pepper**

3 **bay leaves**

1 **teaspoon cumin seeds**

Salt

2 **teaspoons hot pepper sauce**

• 6 to 8 SERVINGS

SAUTÉED GREEN BEANS WITH SUNFLOWER SEEDS

2 tablespoons unsalted butter or margarine

¼ cup diced (½-inch) onion

¼ cup sunflower seeds

1 teaspoon chopped fresh summer savory or ¼ teaspoon dried savory

1 teaspoon chopped fresh basil or ¼ teaspoon dried basil

1 teaspoon chopped fresh

• 4 to 6 SERVINGS

marjoram or ¼ teaspoon dried marjoram

2 cups green beans, cut into 1½-inch lengths and

cooked until crisp-tender

Salt

Freshly ground pepper to taste

This zesty dish tastes remarkably good made with fresh herbs. When using dried herbs, be sure they come from recently opened jars or packages so their flavor and bite will be retained.

■ In a skillet melt the butter over moderate heat, add the onion, and sauté until the pieces are golden. Add the sunflower seeds, savory, basil, and marjoram, and continue to sauté the mixture until the sunflower seeds are golden brown; do not allow to burn. Add the beans, toss the mixture well, and add salt and pepper to taste. Cook the mixture just until the beans are hot. Serve at once.

GREEN BEANS SUPREME

■ Place the beans in a saucepan, add lightly salted water to cover, and bring to a boil over high heat. Lower the heat and cook the beans, uncovered, until they are just tender, 10 to 12 minutes. Drain the beans and return to the saucepan.

In a small bowl, beat the egg yolks with the cream, dill, and savory. Pour the mixture over the beans, place the pan over low heat, and cook the mixture gently, stirring constantly with a wooden spoon, until the sauce is slightly thickened; do not allow the sauce to boil or it will curdle.

Season to taste with salt and pepper, turn out in a serving dish, and dust with the nutmeg. Serve at once.

1 pound green beans, trimmed

Salt

2 egg yolks, lightly beaten

½ cup light cream or half-and-half

1 pinch finely chopped fresh dill

1 pinch finely chopped fresh summer savory or basil

Freshly ground black pepper

1 pinch freshly grated nutmeg

• 4 SERVINGS

QUICK ORIENTAL GREEN BEANS

3 tablespoons corn or peanut oil

1 teaspoon minced fresh ginger

1 teaspoon minced garlic

½ cup sliced canned bamboo shoots, drained

½ cup canned water chestnuts, drained and sliced

• 4 SERVINGS

1 pound fresh green beans, trimmed, cooked until crisp-tender, and drained

1 teaspoon sugar

Salt

Freshly ground black pepper

■ In a wok or heavy skillet, heat the oil over moderately high heat. Stir in the ginger and garlic and stir-fry for 30 seconds. Add the bamboo shoots and water chestnuts and stir-fry for about 1 minute, or until the vegetables are well heated. Add the green beans and sugar. Salt and pepper to taste and continue to cook the mixture for 1 or 2 minutes more, or until the beans are very hot and all the vegetables are well mixed. Serve at once.

BEAN-STUFFED TOMATOES

This is a dish that lends itself to spur-of-the-moment variations. The stuffing can be any cooked bean dish of your choice—we've selected a version of the black bean recipe that opens this chapter—and the toppings can range from shredded Cheddar or Gruyère cheese, to plain or Parmesan cheese-laced bread crumbs, to chopped pignoli nuts or sesame or sunflower seeds. Ripe but firm tomatoes are best; they'll hold their shape when baked. Stuffed tomatoes are always welcome as a side dish or served as a light luncheon main course if served with a salad.

■ With a sharp knife cut a thin slice from the stem ends of the tomatoes and discard them. With a teaspoon scoop out the pulp and seeds, sprinkle the insides of the tomatoes with the salt, and turn the tomatoes upside down on a rack to drain for 30 minutes.

8 large ripe firm tomatoes

1 teaspoon salt

½ recipe Black Bean Purée with Sour Cream (page 116)

1 cup fresh bread crumbs

2 tablespoons chopped parsley or chopped fresh coriander (cilantro)

Olive oil

Sour cream

Prepare the black beans as directed, but instead of processing them to a smooth purée, chop them coarsely in the food processor. Let the beans cool.

Preheat the oven to 375°F. Oil a shallow baking dish large enough to hold all the tomatoes in one layer.

Fill the tomatoes with the bean mixture and place them in the casserole. In a small bowl, toss the bread crumbs with the parsley, divide the mixture among the tomatoes, pressing it gently over the beans. Drizzle a little olive oil over the bread crumbs and bake the tomatoes for about 30 minutes, or until they are cooked but not falling apart. If the crumbs brown too quickly, cover the tops of the tomatoes with foil. Serve hot or at room temperature, topped with sour cream if desired.

• 8 SERVINGS

HAWAIIAN KIDNEY BEAN SAUCE

1 can (1 pound) red kidney beans

⅓ cup water

1 clove garlic, finely chopped

1 cup apricot jam or preserves

1 teaspoon Kitchen Bouquet

1 tablespoon chili powder

½ teaspoon ground cinnamon

½ teaspoon ground cloves

1 pinch ground anise or fennel seed

½ teaspoon salt

1 large pinch freshly grated black pepper

■ Purée the beans in a food processor. Pour the water into a saucepan, add the garlic, jam, Kitchen Bouquet, chili powder, cinnamon, cloves, anise, salt, and pepper and bring to a boil over moderate heat. Cook, stirring constantly, for 5 minutes. Add the bean purée and simmer the sauce gently for 10 minutes, stirring to keep it from sticking to the pan. Pour into a sauceboat and serve hot with rice or with meats and poultry.

• 2 CUPS

135

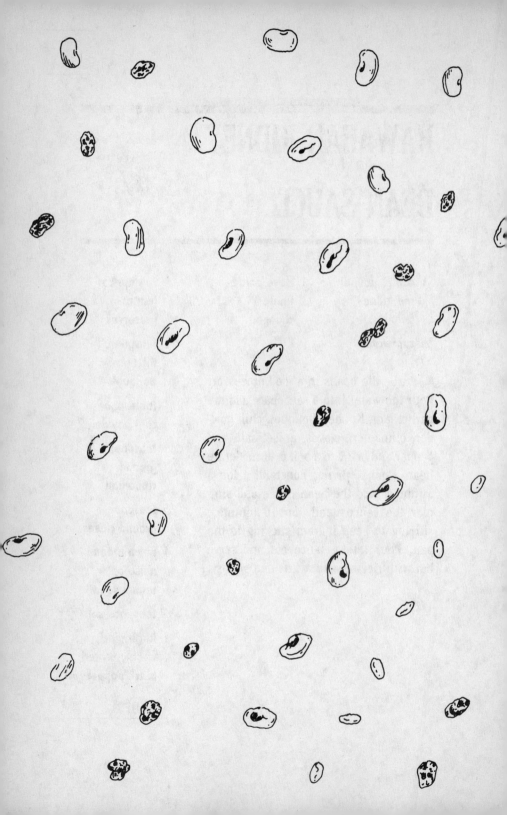

MAIN
COURSES

NEW ENGLAND BAKED

NAVY BEANS

1 quart dried
navy beans,
picked over,
rinsed, and
soaked

1 onion
(optional)

Boiling water

8 ounces salt
pork, with
rind

1 teaspoon dry
mustard

2 teaspoons salt

¼ teaspoon
ground ginger

2 tablespoons
sugar

¼ cup molasses

This is a classic recipe for baked beans; it contains the four basic ingredients—beans, salt pork, spices, and sweetening—and it bakes for many hours in an earthenware pot. This recipe calls for considerably less sweetener —in this case, molasses—than some of the recipes that follow it.

■ Drain the beans, place in a large kettle, and cover with cold water. Bring to a boil over high heat, lower the heat, and simmer the beans, covered, for 30 minutes.

Preheat the oven to 250°F. Drain the beans, rinse them under cold running water, and drain again. Place the onion, if desired, in a 4-quart bean pot or casserole, then add the beans. Place the salt pork in a strainer and pour boiling water over it. With a sharp knife score the rind, making 12-inch incisions, but do not cut through the rind. Press the pork gently into the beans.

In a small bowl, combine the mustard, salt, ginger, sugar, and molasses and mix well. Stir in 1½ cups of boiling water, pour the mixture over the beans, and cover the pot.

Bake for about 9 hours, adding a little boiling water every hour, or when needed, to keep the liquid just below the surface of the beans. Thirty minutes before the end of cooking, remove the cover to allow the beans to form a crust.

**• 6 to 8
SERVINGS**

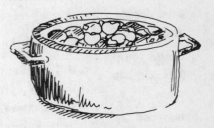

VARIATION For a sweeter and spicier dish, substitute the following mixture for the seasonings, spices, and sweeteners above: 1 teaspoon dry mustard; 2 teaspoons salt; ½ teaspoon freshly ground black pepper; ¾ cup firmly packed dark brown sugar; ½ cup molasses; ½ cup cider vinegar; ½ cup catsup; 1 large apple, peeled, cored, and finely chopped; and 1 cup boiling water. Proceed with the recipe as directed.

EASTMAN FAMILY BAKED BEANS

1 quart dried navy or marrow beans, picked over, rinsed, and soaked

8 ounces salt pork, cut into cubes

½ teaspoon dry mustard

1 teaspoon ground ginger

3 tablespoons salt

1 cup dark brown sugar, maple syrup, or molasses

Boiling water

• 10 to 12 SERVINGS

This recipe has been handed down from generation to generation in the Eastman family for almost two hundred years.

■ Drain and rinse the beans, place them in a large kettle, and cover again with cold water. Bring to boil over high heat, lower the heat, and simmer the beans, covered, until they are tender. (The traditional test is to spoon 2 or 3 beans out of the pot and blow on them; if their skins break, they are tender.) Drain the beans.

Preheat the oven to 350°F. In a large earthenware pot, layer the beans with the salt pork, spices and salt, and the sugar. Add boiling water to just cover the beans and bake, covered, for 6 to 8 hours, adding water from time to time as needed. Remove the cover during the last 45 minutes of baking.

EAST COAST

BAKED NAVY BEANS

■ Drain the beans, place them in a large kettle, and add 2 quarts of water. Bring to a boil over high heat, reduce the heat, and simmer, covered, for 30 minutes. Drain the beans.

Preheat the oven to 300°F. Put the beans in a large casserole or bean pot, add the bacon, and stir until well combined. In a bowl, place the salt, garlic, sugar, mustard, and molasses and mix well. Pour the mixture over the beans and add enough boiling water to cover the beans.

Bake the beans, covered, for 6 hours, stirring occasionally so they will cook evenly. If the mixture is too dry, add more boiling water, but do not drench. Remove the cover 30 minutes before the beans are done to allow the top to brown.

3 cups dried navy beans, picked over, rinsed, and soaked

8 ounces sliced bacon, cut into ½-inch pieces

1 teaspoon salt

1 clove garlic, minced

¼ cup firmly packed light brown sugar

2 teaspoons dry mustard

1 cup dark molasses

Boiling water

• 6 to 8 SERVINGS

HOME-BAKED BEANS, IDAHO STYLE

1 quart great northern beans, picked over, rinsed, and soaked

3 quarts cold water

2 medium onions, 1 of them stuck with 2 whole cloves

1 bay leaf

1 clove garlic

2 tablespoons unsalted butter

8 ounces salt pork

¼ cup firmly packed dark or light brown sugar

■ Drain the beans and place them in a large kettle with the water, the clove-pierced onion, bay leaf, garlic, and butter. Bring the mixture to a boil over high heat, reduce the heat, and simmer the beans, covered, until the skins wrinkle and start to crack, about 45 minutes. Remove the kettle from the heat, discard the onion, bay leaf, and garlic, and drain the beans, reserving the liquid.

Preheat the oven to 250°F. Wash the salt pork and scrape off some of the salt. Score the skin into 1-inch squares. Place the remaining onion in a heavy 4-quart bean pot and cover with the beans. Bury the salt pork in the beans, skin side down. In a mixing bowl combine the brown sugar, mustard, salt, molasses, catsup, and Worcestershire sauce. Measure the reserved bean liquid, add enough water to make 3 cups, and bring to a boil in a saucepan. Stir the brown sugar mixture into the liquid and pour over the beans.

Cover the pot, place on a shallow baking sheet to catch any spillovers, and bake for 7 to 8 hours, adding boiling water as needed to keep the gravy juicy and visible just under the surface of the beans. At the end of cooking, taste for seasoning and with a wooden spoon lift the salt pork to the surface. Bake the beans, uncovered, for 30 minutes more to brown the top. Serve from the pot.

1 teaspoon dry
  mustard

1 teaspoon salt

½ cup light or
  dark molasses

½ cup catsup

½ teaspoon
  Worcestershire
  sauce

• 12 to 14
  SERVINGS

WHOOPEE BEER BEANS

3 cups dried navy
  beans, picked
  over and rinsed

12 ounces salt
   pork, thinly
   sliced

1 quart beer

¾ cup molasses

2 teaspoons dry
  mustard

2 teaspoons salt

¼ cup grated
  onions

■ Place the beans in a large kettle, add cold water to cover, and bring to a boil over high heat. Remove from the heat and allow to stand for 1 hour. Add enough water to cover the beans and return them to a boil. Reduce the heat and simmer the beans, covered, for 1 hour. Drain the beans, reserving the liquid.

Preheat the oven to 275°F. Line the bottom of an earthenware bean pot or heavy casserole with half the salt pork and add the beans to the pot. In a mixing bowl place the beer, molasses, mustard, salt, and onions, blend gently once, and pour the mixture over the beans. Add as much of the reserved bean liquid as needed to barely cover the beans and arrange the remaining salt pork over the top. Cover the pot and bake for 7 hours, adding the remaining bean liquid or water as needed to keep the beans barely covered. Remove the cover during the last hour of baking to allow the top to brown.

• 10 to 12
SERVINGS

BETTER BAKED BEANS

This is just one of many recipes ingenious cooks have used to enhance the flavor of canned baked beans. For a sweeter dish add molasses. maple sugar, or brown sugar. For spicier beans add more mustard, chili sauce, or hot pepper sauce.

■ Preheat the oven to 350°F. Place the beans in casserole and set aside.

In a skillet melt the butter over moderate heat, add the onion, and brown it, stirring often to prevent it from burning. Stir in the mustard, catsup, and wine and blend until smooth. Pour the mixture over the beans and stir gently.

Make a lattice of bacon over the top of the beans and bake them until the bacon is brown, about 40 minutes. Serve very hot accompanied by the wine used in the casserole.

1 can (2 pounds) baked beans

1 tablespoon unsalted butter

1 small Bermuda onion, finely chopped

1 teaspoon dry mustard

¼ cup catsup

¼ cup dry white wine

8 strips bacon

• 4 SERVINGS

BEAN AND BEEF BAKE

3 slices bacon,
cut into
thirds

2 cups thinly
sliced onion

8 ounces lean
ground beef

1⅔ cups canned
pork and
beans with
tomato
sauce

½ cup catsup

2 tablespoons
molasses

1 teaspoon
salt

Freshly
ground black
pepper

■ Preheat the oven to 350°F. In a skillet, fry the bacon over moderately low heat until crisp. Drain the bacon on paper towels. Add the onion and ground beef to the skillet, raise the heat to moderate, and cook until the onion and beef are browned, breaking up the beef with a wooden spoon. Add the pork and beans, catsup, molasses, salt, and pepper to taste and stir until well combined. Transfer the mixture to a 1½-quart baking dish and bake, uncovered, for 1 hour. Serve very hot.

• 4 SERVINGS

BLACK BEANS IN RUM

4 tablespoons
(½ stick)
unsalted butter

¾ cup finely
chopped
onion

2 tablespoons
minced garlic

½ cup chopped
celery

¼ cup chopped
carrot

¼ cup chopped
parsley

1 bay leaf

1 teaspoon
dried thyme
leaves

2 cups cooked
black beans,
drained

¼ cup dark rum

¾ cup sour
cream

■ In a skillet melt the butter over moderately low heat, add the onion, garlic, celery, carrot, parsley, bay leaf, and thyme and sauté the mixture slowly until the vegetables are soft, 5 to 6 minutes. Remove and discard the bay leaf. Add the beans, and cook, stirring until they are very hot. Stir in the rum and heat 30 seconds more. Serve the beans in heated bowls, topped with a dollop of sour cream.

• 6 SERVINGS

PICADILLO WITH RICE AND BEANS

BLACK BEAN MIXTURE

1 tablespoon vegetable oil

¼ cup finely chopped onion

1 tablespoon minced garlic

¼ cup chopped smoked ham

2 cups cooked, drained black beans

Salt

Freshly ground black pepper

Drops of hot pepper sauce

ROAST BEEF MIXTURE

2 cups diced (¼-inch) lean roast beef

2 cups peeled, seeded, and diced tomato

½ cup coarsely chopped onion

¼ cup diced green bell pepper

1 teaspoon capers, drained

2 tablespoons unsalted butter

3 or 4 bananas, halved lengthwise

6 cups hot steamed rice

¼ cup chopped hard-cooked egg

Every Latin American country has its own version, or versions, of picadillo, a hash usually made with ground beef. In this unusual interpretation, the black

beans become the hash and the beef
(roast beef, in this case) becomes part
of a sauce.

■ To make the black bean mixture,
heat the oil in a skillet over moderate
heat, add the onion, garlic, and ham,
and sauté until the onions are golden.
Add the black beans. Salt and pepper to
taste. Add the hot pepper sauce, mix
well, and keep the mixture hot.

To make the roast beef mixture, in a
mixing bowl combine the roast beef, tomato, onion, green pepper, and capers.

In another skillet, heat the butter,
add the bananas and sauté until golden
brown on both sides. Keep the bananas
hot.

To assemble the dish, spread the rice
evenly on a large, heated platter, then
spread the bean mixture on top of it.
Make a final layer of the roast beef
sauce and sprinkle it with the chopped
egg. Arrange the sautéed bananas
around the edge of the platter and serve
at once.

**• 6 to 8
SERVINGS**

BLACK BEANS, PORK, AND RICE

1½ cups dried black beans, rinsed, picked over, and soaked

¼ cup olive or salad oil

1 clove garlic, finely chopped

1 large onion, finely chopped

1 green bell pepper, chopped

Freshly ground pepper

Salt

1 pound lean pork, cut into ½-inch cubes

½ pound pork sausages, cut into ½-inch pieces

½ cup fresh orange juice

½ cup dry red wine

2 cups hot cooked rice

2 tablespoons chopped parsley or fresh coriander (cilantro; optional)

6 slices orange, with rind

■ Drain and rinse the beans. In a large heavy saucepan heat the olive oil over moderate heat, stir in the garlic, onion, and green pepper, and sauté until the onion is lightly browned. Add the beans, ¼ teaspoon of black pepper, and enough water to cover the mixture. Bring the water to a boil, lower the heat, and simmer the mixture 1½ to 2 hours, or until the beans are tender. Add water as necessary to keep the mixture from sticking to the bottom of the skillet. Season the beans with salt to taste. In a food processor purée 1 cup of the beans with a little of the liquid and reserve the purée.

Place the pork and sausages in a cold skillet, set over moderate heat, and sauté until the meats are golden brown on all sides, stirring often. Drain off the fat, add the orange juice and wine, season to taste with salt and pepper, and simmer the mixture gently for 5 minutes. Remove the meats from the sauce and set aside. Add the puréed beans to the sauce and simmer 5 minutes more.

To assemble the dish, reheat the beans if necessary. Distribute the rice around the rim of a shallow serving bowl and ladle the beans into the center. Arrange the meats over the beans, sprinkle the top with parsley, if desired, and place the orange slices around the edge of the dish. Serve the sauce separately in a sauceboat.

• **4 to 6
SERVINGS**

CHEDDAR CHEESE AND BLACK BEAN LOAF

1 tablespoon unsalted butter

¼ cup finely chopped onion

¼ teaspoon dried thyme leaves

2 cups cooked black beans, drained

1 cup fresh bread crumbs

1 large egg, well beaten

Salt

Freshly ground black pepper

1 cup grated sharp Cheddar cheese

A great cold-weather dish. For extra color and texture, you might sauté chopped garlic, bell pepper, and celery with the onion—but add a little extra butter if you do.

■ Preheat the oven to 350°F and grease a shallow 1½-quart baking dish. In a small skillet, melt the butter over moderate heat, add the onion and thyme, and sauté until the onion is translucent, about 3 to 5 minutes. Transfer the mixture to a mixing bowl, add the beans, bread crumbs, and egg, and mix thoroughly. Add salt and pepper to taste and turn the mixture into the baking dish. Sprinkle the top of the loaf with the cheese and bake for 45 minutes, or until the loaf puffs up and is firm to the touch and the cheese is brown.

• 4 to 6 SERVINGS

BLACK-EYED PEAS
WITH GINGER

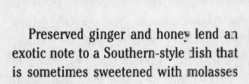

Preserved ginger and honey lend an exotic note to a Southern-style dish that is sometimes sweetened with molasses or brown sugar.

■ Drain and rinse the beans, cover with fresh water, and bring to a boil over high heat. Reduce the heat and simmer the beans, covered, for 45 minutes to 1 hour, or until tender, adding water as necessary to keep the beans juicy.

Preheat the oven to 325°F. In a skillet sauté the onion and bacon over moderate heat until the onion is golden and the bacon is crisp, stirring often. Drain off the fat. Stir the onions and bacon into the beans and add mustard. Salt and pepper to taste. Add ginger, and combine well. Turn the beans into a deep 2-quart baking dish and drizzle the honey over the top. Bake, covered, 1½ hours, removing the cover after 1 hour to brown the top.

2 cups dried black-eyed peas, picked over, rinsed, and soaked

1 onion, finely chopped

6 slices bacon, cut into 1-inch squares

1 teaspoon dry mustard

Salt

Freshly ground black pepper

¼ cup preserved ginger, chopped

¾ cup honey

• 4 SERVINGS

BLACK-EYED
PEAS AND BACON

1 pound dried black-eyed peas, picked over, rinsed, and soaked

8 ounces bacon, finely chopped

3 onions, finely chopped

1 clove garlic, minced

4 small red chili peppers, seeded and finely chopped (use rubber gloves) or 5 black peppercorns, crushed

½ cup white wine

■ Drain and rinse the beans and return to the pan, add the bacon, onions, garlic, chili peppers, and cold water to cover. Bring to a boil over high heat, reduce heat, and simmer the mixture, covered, 45 minutes, or until the beans are just tender. Stir in the white wine and simmer until the beans are very tender, adding water as necessary to keep the beans juicy. Serve with rice.

• 4 to 6
SERVINGS

BLACK-EYED PEA LOAF

2 tablespoons vegetable oil

½ cup finely chopped onion

1 teaspoon curry powder

2 cups cooked dried black-eyed peas, drained

⅓ cup raw rolled oats

½ cup yellow corn meal

2 cups vegetable or chicken stock

Salt

Freshly ground white pepper

■ Preheat the oven to 350°F. Grease a 9-inch loaf pan.

In a large skillet, heat the oil over moderate heat, add the onion, and sauté until the onion is golden. Add the curry powder and stir 1 to 2 minutes more. Add the black-eyed peas, rolled oats, cornmeal, and stock, and stir well.

Turn the mixture into the loaf pan and bake for 45 minutes, or until the oats and cornmeal are cooked and have absorbed all the liquid. The consistency should be that of a very thick gruel. Stir in salt and pepper to taste and press the mixture firmly in the pan.

Cool and then chill the loaf. Cut into slices and eat cold, or fry in vegetable oil or butter as you would corn meal mush or scrapple.

• 4 to 6
SERVINGS

QUICK CHILI CON CARNE WITH BEANS

1½ pounds
ground beef
chuck

1 cup chopped
onion

½ cup diced
(¼-inch)
green bell
pepper

1 tablespoon
chili powder

1 teaspoon
salt

1 can (10-ounce)
tomato soup

2 cups canned
tomatoes,
diced and
with their
juices

2 cups canned
kidney
beans, drained

1 teaspoon
garlic
powder

• 3 to 4
SERVINGS

The words *quick* and *chili* are seldom paired in the Southwest, nor is the use of canned tomato soup considered respectable. But what can we say? As long as we're flying in the face of Southwestern custom, why not go all the way and make an easy dish of it.

■ In a large, cold, saucepan put the beef, onion, green pepper, chili powder, and salt, and place over moderate heat. Sauté, breaking up the meat with a wooden spoon and mixing together all the ingredients, until the beef is cooked throughout. (The beef will render enough fat to prevent the onion and pepper from sticking.)

Add the soup, tomatoes, kidney beans, and garlic powder, mix well, and simmer, uncovered, until the chili has the consistency you prefer. Serve hot with steamed rice and soda crackers.

CHILI CON CARNE, SUN VALLEY STYLE

1 quart dried pinto or red beans, picked over, rinsed, and soaked

3 quarts water

1 large onion

1 large clove garlic, thinly sliced

1 tablespoon unsalted butter

1 large bay leaf

4 teaspoons salt

2 tablespoons suet or vegetable oil

2 pounds lean ground beef

1 cup water, beef stock, or tomato juice

4 tablespoons chili powder

1½ teaspoons ground cumin

■ Drain the beans, place them in a large, heavy kettle with the water, onion, garlic, butter, and bay leaf, and bring to a boil over high heat. Reduce the heat and simmer the mixture, covered, for 2 hours, or until the beans are just tender.

In a skillet, melt the suet over moderately high heat, add the beef, and brown it quickly, breaking it up into small pieces with a wooden spoon. Add the beef to the beans. Add the water to the skillet and bring it to a boil, stirring up all the browned bits of meat, then pour the liquid into the bean pot.

In a cup, blend the chili powder and cumin with a little of the bean liquid and mix to a smooth paste. Stir the paste into the beans, bring the mixture to a boil, then cover and simmer for 1½ hours. Serve the chili in heated soup plates.

• 10 SERVINGS

TEX-MEX CHILI

2 cups dried pinto beans, picked over, rinsed, and soaked

Salt

1 tablespoon bacon drippings

2 pounds beef chuck, very coarsely ground or cut into ⅜-inch dice

1 cup diced (¼-inch) onions

3 tablespoons chili powder

1 tablespoon cumin seeds, crushed

1 teaspoon sugar

Freshly ground black pepper

2 cups solid-pack tomatoes

■ Drain the beans, place them in a large saucepan, and add cold water to cover. Bring to a boil over high heat, lower heat, and simmer the beans, covered, until they are tender, 1½ to 2 hours. Add salt to taste and reserve.

In a large, heavy kettle, heat the bacon drippings over moderate heat and add the beef, onions, chili powder, cumin seeds, sugar, and 1 tablespoon of salt. Add pepper to taste. Sauté the mixture, breaking up the beef with a wooden spoon, until all the ingredients are well mixed and the beef shows no traces of pink. Add the tomatoes, crushing the fruit with the spoon, then add the beans and simmer the chili, covered, until it reaches the consistency you wish, around 30 minutes. Serve hot over steamed rice.

• 10 to 12
SERVINGS

MEATLESS KIDNEY BEAN CHILI

3 tablespoons vegetable oil

1½ cups diced (¼-inch) onions

1½ tablespoons minced garlic

2 tablespoons dried oregano

2 teaspoons ground cumin

2 teaspoons chili powder

6 cups cooked red kidney beans, drained

2 cups peeled, seeded, and chopped tomatoes or drained canned plum tomatoes, lightly crushed

2 cups vegetable stock or water

1 tablespoon fresh lemon juice

¼ teaspoon cayenne pepper

Salt

Freshly ground black pepper

A hearty, satisfying chili, although Texans might not think so because of the "practically illicit" beans that are the major ingredient.

■ In a large, heavy kettle, heat the oil over moderate heat, add the onions, garlic, oregano, cumin, and chili powder, and sauté until the onions are translucent. Add the beans, tomatoes, stock, lemon juice, and cayenne. Salt and pepper to taste. Mix well, and bring to a boil over low heat. Reduce the heat and simmer the chili, uncovered, until it thickens slightly, about 30 minutes. Taste the chili to see if it's spicy enough and serve over steamed rice.

• 8 to 10 SERVINGS

CHILI BEEF BALLS

AND PINTO BEANS

2 cups dried
pinto beans,
picked over,
rinsed, and
soaked

2 pounds ground
round steak

6 tablespoons
(¾ stick)
unsalted
butter

1 large Spanish
onion, coarsely
chopped

3 cups beef
bouillon

1 teaspoon salt

1 tablespoon
chili powder

½ teaspoon finely
chopped fresh
oregano or 1 small
pinch dried oregano

1 tablespoon
chopped
parsley

• **6 SERVINGS**

■ Drain the pinto beans, place them in a saucepan with water to cover, and bring to a boil over high heat. Reduce the heat and simmer the beans, covered, until they are tender, 1½ to 2 hours. Drain the beans and place in a 3-quart casserole.

Preheat the oven to 350°F. While the beans are cooking, form the ground beef into balls 1 inch in diameter. In a large skillet, melt the butter over moderate heat. Sauté the meatballs in batches until browned on all sides.

In the same skillet sauté the onions until they are golden brown. Add the bouillon, salt, chili powder, and oregano and simmer, uncovered, for 20 minutes. Pour the sauce over the beans and arrange the meatballs over the top. Sprinkle with parsley and bake the chili, uncovered, for 20 minutes, or until the flavors are blended. Serve from the casserole and accompany with steamed rice.

SPICY CRANBERRY BEANS

1 pound dried cranberry beans, picked over, rinsed, and soaked

6 cups water

1 medium onion, thinly sliced

4 ounces salt pork, cut into ¼-inch dice

1 teaspoon whole cloves, tied in a cheesecloth bag

1 can (8 ounces) tomato sauce

1 tablespoon Worcestershire sauce

2 tablespoons molasses

Salt

■ Drain and rinse the beans, place them in a large saucepan with the water, onion, salt pork, and cloves and bring to a boil over high heat. Lower the heat and simmer the mixture, covered, until the beans are tender, about 2 hours. Stir the beans occasionally and add water, if necessary.

Remove the bag of cloves and add the tomato sauce, Worcestershire sauce, molasses, and salt to taste. Stir gently and simmer 30 minutes longer.

• 6 SERVINGS

GARBANZO BEANS AND CHICKEN

1½ teaspoons salt

¼ teaspoon ground ginger

1 3-pound frying chicken, cut into 8 pieces

6 tablespoons (¾ stick) unsalted butter

2 cups finely chopped onions

2½ cups cooked garbanzos, drained

1 teaspoon ground cumin

1 tablespoon ground coriander

• 4 to 6 SERVINGS

¾ teaspoon freshly ground black pepper

1½ cups chicken broth

■ Mix the salt and ginger and rub the mixture into the chicken pieces. In a large, heavy skillet, melt 2 tablespoons of the butter over moderate heat. Add some of the chicken pieces and brown them on all sides, removing them to a platter as they brown. Continue browning the chicken, adding butter as needed. Add the onions to the skillet and sauté them until they are lightly browned. Return the chicken to the skillet, add the garbanzos, cumin, coriander, and black pepper, and mix well. Cover the skillet, reduce the heat to low, and cook the mixture for 15 minutes, shaking the pan frequently.

Stir in the broth, cover the skillet, and simmer the mixture 30 minutes, removing the cover during the last 10 minutes of cooking to reduce the liquid. There should be very little gravy left when the dish is ready. Serve very hot.

CURRIED QUICHE WITH GARBANZOS AND GREEN BEANS

1 tablespoon vegetable oil or unsalted butter

½ cup finely chopped onion

1 teaspoon minced garlic

1½ cups cooked garbanzos, drained

1 cup green beans, cooked until crisp-tender

2 tablespoons chopped parsley

1½ teaspoons curry powder

1 pinch dry mustard

Salt

Freshly ground black pepper

4 large eggs, beaten

1 9-inch unbaked pie shell

1 cup shredded Monterey Jack cheese

■ Preheat the oven to 350°F. Heat the oil in a small skillet over moderate heat, add the onion and garlic, and sauté until the onion is golden. Transfer the mixture to a bowl, add the garbanzos, green beans, parsley, curry powder, and mustard. Salt and pepper to taste, and add the eggs. Mix well and pour into the pie shell. Sprinkle the cheese on top and bake the pie for 40 to 50 minutes. Serve hot or warm.

• 6 to 8 SERVINGS

SPINACH AND POTATO PIE

2½ cups firm mashed potatoes

1 cup frozen chopped spinach, thawed and squeezed dry

¼ cup puréed cooked garbanzos

1¼ cups buttermilk

1 teaspoon chopped fresh basil or ¼ teaspoon dried basil

1 teaspoon chopped fresh thyme or ¼ teaspoon dried thyme leaves

An Americanized Greek dish that combines some of the best features of *boreka, spanakopeta,* and other Greek specialties. To carry through the theme, you might want to serve retsina instead of your usual dry white wine. This is an attractive dish to make ahead for a buffet dinner.

■ Preheat the oven to 350°F. In a mixing bowl combine the potatoes, spinach, garbanzos, buttermilk, basil, thyme, and nutmeg and mix well.

Brush a 9 × 12 inch or 9 × 13 inch baking pan with some of the butter, using a pastry brush. With a sharp knife, cut the filo dough to measure the dimensions of the pan and follow the package instructions for keeping the pastry from drying out while you assemble the pie.

Brush 1 layer of the dough with the melted butter and lay it flat in the pan. Brush another sheet of filo with butter, place it over the first sheet, and top with a third, unbuttered sheet.

Using a rubber spatula, spread some of the potato mixture over the dough, bringing it to the edge of the pan. Butter and layer 3 more layers of filo and spread with another layer of the potato mixture. Continue making layers of buttered filo and filling. Sprinkle the final layer of filling with the cheese.

Bake for about 30 minutes, or until the pie is heated through and the top is nicely browned.

¼ teaspoon freshly grated nutmeg

4 to 6 tablespoons (½ to ¾ stick) unsalted butter, melted

1 package (1 pound) frozen filo dough, thawed

4 ounces feta cheese, crumbled

• 8 SERVINGS

LENTILS CREOLE

1 cup dried lentils

2 teaspoons salt

2 tablespoons unsalted butter or margarine

1 onion, finely chopped

2 green bell peppers, finely chopped

2 cups canned tomatoes

¼ teaspoon freshly ground black pepper

1 teaspoon sugar

Cooked rice or noodles

■ In a saucepan, place the lentils, water to cover, and the salt, and bring to a boil over high heat. Reduce the heat and simmer the lentils, covered, until they are very tender, about 1 hour. Drain the lentils and reserve.

In another saucepan, melt the butter over moderate heat, add the onion and green peppers, and sauté until the onion begins to brown. Add the tomatoes, black pepper, sugar, and lentils, and bring to a simmer. Simmer the mixture, covered, for 30 to 40 minutes, or until the lentils are mushy. Serve over rice or noodles.

• 4 SERVINGS

LENTIL AND

PORK CASSEROLE

2½ cups lentils, picked over and rinsed

1 onion pierced with 3 whole cloves

1 bay leaf

Salt

■ Place lentils in a kettle with the onion, bay leaf, and 1 teaspoon of salt, cover with cold water, and bring to a boil. Reduce the heat and simmer the lentils until they are tender but still firm, about 35 minutes, taking care not to overcook them. Remove the onion and bay leaf and drain the lentils, reserving the liquid.

Meanwhile, place the pork chops in a cold skillet, place over moderate heat, and brown the chops on both sides. Season them to taste with salt and pepper.

Preheat the oven to 350°F. Spread half the lentils on the bottom of a shallow baking dish. Place the pork chops over the lentils and cover the chops with the remaining lentils. Pour the lentil liquid over the top and bake for 1 hour. Add boiling water, if necessary, to keep the mixture moist.

Make a lattice of the bacon strips and place over the lentils during the last 20 minutes of baking to brown until crisp. Serve from the baking dish.

6 thick loin pork chops

Freshly ground black pepper

6 bacon strips

• 6 SERVINGS

VARIATIONS

LENTIL AND ROAST DUCK: Melt 3 tablespoons unsalted butter in a skillet, add ¼ cup finely chopped onion, and sauté until the onions are golden. Add 2 tablespoons chopped parsley and ¼ teaspoon dried thyme and stir the mixture into the lentils. Layer the lentils with 6 slices or pieces of cold roast duck. Blend the reserved lentil liquid with 1 cup of red wine and pour over the casserole. Bake as directed.

LENTIL AND VIRGINIA HAM: Layer 6 thin slices of baked Virginia ham with the lentils. Add 1 teaspoon dry mustard to the lentil liquid before pouring it over the lentils and ham.

SPICY LENTIL AND HAM: Melt 2 tablespoons unsalted butter in a small skillet, add ½ cup finely chopped onion and 1 clove garlic, minced, and sauté until the onion is golden. Stir the onion mixture into the cooked lentils along with 1½ cups diced cooked ham, 2 tablespoons chopped parsely, and ½ teaspoon dried thyme. Blend the mixture well and transfer it to a baking dish. Add ½ cup red wine to the lentil liquid and pour it over the lentil-ham mixture. Bake as directed, adding additional red wine as needed.

LENTILS AND SALAMI: Layer one-third of the cooked lentils with thinly sliced salami, cover with half the remaining lentils and make another layer of salami. Finish with the remaining lentils and top with the bacon-strip lattice. Bake for 30 minutes only.

LENTILS AND HOT SAUSAGE: Layer the cooked lentils with 6 Italian or Spanish hot sausages that have been browned but not cooked through and bake as directed. Twenty minutes before removing the dish from the oven sprinkle the top with ¼ cup freshly grated Parmesan cheese.

LENTILS AND PORK SAUSAGE: Layer the cooked lentils with 12 pork sausages that have been parboiled for 10 minutes. Add a layer of thinly sliced salami, if you wish. Bake as directed.

LENTIL AND BRAZIL NUT LOAF

■ Preheat the oven to 350°F and butter an 8-inch loaf pan or 1-quart baking dish. In a skillet, melt the butter over moderate heat, add the onion, and sauté until it is golden brown. Transfer the onions to a mixing bowl, add the lentils, nuts, bread crumbs, sage, salt, and egg, and mix very well.

Turn into the prepared pan and bake for 45 minutes, or until browned on top and cooked through. Serve the loaf hot or cold.

8 tablespoons (1 stick) unsalted butter

½ cup finely chopped onion

2 cups cooked lentils, drained

¾ cup chopped Brazil nuts

1 cup soft bread crumbs

½ teaspoon dried sage leaves

1 teaspoon salt

1 large egg, beaten

• 6 to 8 SERVINGS

FRESH LIMA BEANS
AND PORK CHOPS

8 thick pork chops

3 tablespoons unsalted butter

2 large onions, finely chopped

2 cups long grain rice

2 tomatoes, peeled, seeded, and chopped

2 cups fresh or thawed frozen lima beans

6 cups chicken broth

1 bay leaf

1 pinch rosemary

• 6 to 8 SERVINGS

Salt

Freshly ground black pepper

1 tablespoon finely chopped parsley

■ Place the pork chops in a large heavy skillet. Set the pan over moderate heat, and fry the meat until it is golden brown on all sides. Remove the chops from the pan, cut the meat from the bone, discarding the bones, and cut the meat into bite-size pieces.

Add the butter to the skillet and let it melt. Add the onions and rice and sauté them until the rice looks chalky. Add the tomatoes, lima beans, reserved pork, chicken broth, bay leaf, and rosemary. Salt and pepper to taste. Stir to mix all the ingredients well and bring to a boil. Reduce the heat and simmer the mixture, covered, for 30 minutes without stirring. Fluff the rice with a fork and transfer the stew to a platter. Sprinkle with parsley and serve at once.

BEEF AND LIMA BEAN PILAF

4 pounds round steak

2 cloves garlic, split

6 teaspoons salt

1 teaspoon freshly ground black pepper

¼ cup chili powder

¼ cup prepared mustard

1 quart large dried lima beans, picked over, rinsed, and soaked

¼ cup vegetable oil

4 large onions, finely chopped

2 cups long-grain rice

2 cups canned tomatoes

1 cup sliced pitted ripe olives

4 cans (10 ½ ounces each) beef bouillon

■ Preheat the oven to 350°F. You will need 2 large casseroles.

Rub the steak all over with the cut surfaces of the garlic, then sprinkle with 2 teaspoons of the salt, the pepper, and chili powder and rub the seasonings in well. Spread the top of the steak with the mustard, cut the beef into 1-inch squares, and reserve. Drain the dried beans and reserve.

In a large skillet, heat the oil over moderate heat, add the onions and rice, and cook, stirring occasionally, until the onions are golden and the rice looks chalky.

Layer the ingredients in each casserole as follows: one-quarter each of the meat squares, onion-rice mixture, to-matoes, and beans, then sprinkle with one-quarter of the remaining salt, pepper, and chili powder; repeat the layers. Each casserole should be only two-thirds full to allow room for the beans and rice to expand as they cook. Pour in as much beef bouillon as the casserole will hold, adding water, if necessary.

Bake for about 3 hours, or until the beans are tender, adding more bouillon or water to keep the mixture from becoming too dry.

• 30 SERVINGS

LIMA BEANS WITH SOUR CREAM

1 pound dried lima beans, picked over, rinsed, and soaked

2 tablespoons maple syrup

1½ teaspoons dry mustard

1 cup sour cream

Salt

Freshly ground black pepper

6 strips bacon, fried crisp,

drained, and crumbled

¼ teaspoon dried thyme

¼ teaspoon dried rosemary

■ Preheat the oven to 350°F. Drain the beans, place in a heavy saucepan with water to cover, and bring to a boil over high heat. Reduce the heat and simmer the beans, covered, until they are tender, about 1 hour.

Drain the beans and place in a 1½-quart baking dish. In a small bowl, stir into a paste the syrup, mustard, and sour cream. Salt and pepper to taste. Add the mixture to the beans and combine gently. Sprinkle the top with the bacon and herbs and bake, uncovered, for 30 minutes.

• 4 SERVINGS

LIMA BEANS AND SHORT RIBS

1 cup large dried lima beans, picked over, rinsed, and soaked

4 medium onions, quartered

4⅔ cups water

1 teaspoon salt

1 teaspoon dried sage

3 tablespoons all-purpose flour

Freshly ground black pepper

1 teaspoon dry mustard

2 pounds beef short ribs, cut into 2-inch pieces

Vegetable oil

■ Drain the lima beans, place them in a saucepan with the onions and 4 cups of the water, and bring to a boil over high heat. Reduce the heat and simmer the beans, covered, for 45 minutes. Add ½ teaspoon of the salt and the sage and simmer for 15 minutes more, or until the beans are tender. Pour the beans and onions, undrained, into a large casserole.

Preheat the oven to 350°F. In a small bowl mix together the remaining salt, flour, black pepper to taste, and the mustard and dredge the short ribs with the mixture. In a heavy skillet, heat the oil over moderately high heat, add the short ribs, in batches, and brown on all sides. Return all the meat to the skillet, reduce the heat to moderately low, cover the pot, and cook the beef, covered, 20 minutes longer. Place the short ribs on top of the limas in the casserole. Sprinkle the drippings in the skillet with the remaining 1 tablespoon of flour and cook over moderate heat until the flour is lightly browned. Stir in the remaining ⅔ cup of water and cook, stirring up the browned bits of meat with a wooden spoon, until the sauce is thickened. Pour the sauce over the short ribs, cover the casserole, and bake for 1½ to 2 hours, or until the meat is very tender. Serve from the casserole.

• 4 SERVINGS

BUTTER BEANS AND LAMB

1 whole shoulder of lamb (3 to 4 pounds)

1 onion, sliced

½ lemon, sliced

1 teaspoon dried mint leaves

6 black peppercorns, crushed

1 cup dry white wine

2 tablespoons olive oil

1½ cups dried lima beans, picked over, rinsed, and soaked

1 cup water

2 teaspoons salt

2 tablespoons all-purpose flour (optional)

Butter beans are another name for lima beans, which when cooked in this simple and sophisticated dish are indeed as luscious as butter, but a lot better for you.

■ Trim the fat from the shoulder of lamb. Place the lamb in a large glass or stainless steel bowl, and cover it with the onion and lemon slices. Sprinkle the top with the mint and peppercorns, and pour the wine over all. Cover the bowl with foil or plastic wrap and let the lamb marinate for 3 to 4 hours at room temperature, turning it occasionally.

Drain the lamb, reserving the marinade, and pat the meat dry with paper towels. Heat the olive oil in a Dutch oven over moderate heat. Add the lamb and brown it on all sides. Drain the lima beans and add them to the lamb with the marinade and water. Cover the Dutch oven and simmer the dish for 2 hours, or until the meat and lima beans are very tender, adding the salt after 1 hour of cooking. Add more water if needed to keep the gravy very juicy.

If you wish a thicker gravy, mix the flour with 2 to 3 tablespoons of cold water in a cup and stir the mixture slowly into the pot until the liquid has thickened.

• 6 SERVINGS

GREEN BEANS AND BEEF IN MUSTARD SAUCE

1½ pounds green beans, trimmed

1 pound bone-less beef sirloin, cut ¾-inch thick

1 cup water

¼ cup Dijon-style mustard

2 teaspoons cornstarch

■ Cook the green beans in a large quantity of boiling water, or steam them, until crisp-tender. Drain the beans, if necessary, and rinse them under cold running water to set the color and stop them from cooking.

Cut the beef into 1-inch cubes and set aside. In a small bowl, mix the water, mustard, cornstarch, salt, and pepper and reserve. In a heavy skillet, heat the oil over moderate heat, add the onion, and sauté until it is slightly wilted. Raise the heat to moderately

MAIN
COURSES

high, add the beef, and cook it until it is brown on all sides but still pink inside, turning often. Stir in the mustard mixture and cook until it is slightly thickened, stirring constantly. Remove the beef from the pan with a slotted spoon and keep it warm in a bowl.

Add the green beans to the skillet and toss until they are heated through and coated with the sauce. Arrange the beans on half of a large platter, spread the lettuce out on the other half, and spoon the beef over it. Serve at once with steamed rice.

1 teaspoon
  salt

¼ teaspoon
  freshly ground
  black pepper

2 tablespoons
  vegetable oil

1 small onion,
  chopped

  Lettuce
  leaves

• 4 SERVINGS

MOLLY'S SPINACH AND GREEN BEAN CASSEROLE

2 teaspoons vegetable oil

1 package (10 ounces) frozen leaf spinach, thawed and well drained

1 package (10 ounces) frozen green beans, thawed

1½ cups chopped zucchini

1 large onion

1 clove garlic, minced

1½ tablespoons chopped

fresh basil or 1½ teaspoons dried basil

⅛ teaspoon freshly grated nutmeg

(cont.)

1½ teaspoons
salt

⅛ teaspoon
freshly
ground black
pepper

¼ cup water

4 large eggs

¼ cup freshly
grated
Parmesan
cheese

• 4 to 6
SERVINGS

■ In a large skillet, heat the oil over moderate heat, add the spinach, and sauté 2 to 3 minutes. Add the zucchini, green beans, onion, garlic, basil, nutmeg, salt, pepper, and water, cover the skillet, and simmer the mixture 10 minutes, stirring occasionally. Remove from the heat, remove the cover, and cool the vegetables until they are lukewarm.

Preheat the oven to 350°F. Beat the eggs in a large mixing bowl, add the vegetables, and turn the mixture into a shallow 2½- to 3-quart baking dish. Place the dish in a larger baking pan and add enough boiling water to the larger pan to come 1 inch up the sides of the smaller baking dish. Bake the spinach–green bean mixture for 25 minutes, or until set. Sprinkle with the cheese and serve at once.

PINK BUCK BEANS

2 cups dried pink beans, picked over, rinsed, and soaked

8 ounces smoked ham, cut into ½-inch cubes, or slab bacon or salt pork cut into 1-inch segments just to the rind

6 cups water

2 medium Bermuda onions, coarsely chopped

2 cloves garlic, thinly sliced

2 cups canned solid-pack tomatoes

½ cup chopped red or green bell pepper (optional)

2 teaspoons chili powder

2 tablespoons dark brown sugar

½ teaspoon dry mustard

½ teaspoon crushed dried oregano or ¼ teaspoon ground cumin

Salt

Freshly ground pepper

Navy beans and pinto beans are excellent substitutes for pink beans in this easily prepared make-ahead recipe, although both need to cook a little longer than pink beans. Add more chili powder and cumin for a more pronounced Mexican flavor.

■ Drain the beans and place them in a large saucepan with the ham, water, onions, garlic, and bay leaf. Bring to a boil over high heat, reduce the heat, and simmer the mixture, covered, for 1½ hours.

Stir in the tomatoes, breaking them up with a spoon, the bell pepper, chili powder, brown sugar, mustard, and oregano. Salt and pepper to taste. Return the mixture to a boil, lower the heat, and simmer the beans for about 15 minutes. Serve with steamed rice.

• 6 SERVINGS

PINK BEANS WITH BACON

1½ cups dried pink beans, picked over, rinsed, and soaked

2 tablespoons butter or meat drippings

1 cup canned tomatoes

1 teaspoon molasses

1 medium onion, finely chopped

1½ teaspoons salt

⅛ teaspoon freshly ground black pepper

3 or 4 thin slices bacon or salt pork

■ Drain the beans, put them into a saucepan with water to cover, and bring to a boil. Lower the heat and simmer the beans for 1½ to 2 hours, or until they are very tender. Stir in 1 teaspoon of salt during the last 15 minutes of cooking. Drain the beans and place them in a 1½-quart casserole.

Preheat the oven to 375°F. Add to the beans the tomatoes, molasses, onion, remaining ½ teaspoon salt, and pepper and mix well. Cover the casserole and bake the mixture for 1 hour.

While the beans are baking, blanch the bacon for 2 minutes in a pan of boiling water and drain on paper towels. Lay the slices over the beans, return the casserole to the oven, and continue baking, uncovered, until the bacon is brown and crisp.

• 4 SERVINGS

RED BEANS
COUNTRY-STYLE

1 pound dried Idaho red bean or red kidney beans, picked over, rinsed, and soaked

6 cups water

2 tablespoons unsalted butter or vegetable oil

8 ounces bulk pork sausage

1 cup coarsely chopped onions

2 cloves garlic mashed with 2 teaspoons salt in a mortar and pestle

2 cups thinly sliced peeled tart apples

¼ teaspoon freshly ground black pepper

1 teaspoon chili powder

1 teaspoon dry mustard

¼ cup firmly packed light or dark brown sugar

1½ cups tomato juice

¼ cup Jamaica rum

Sour cream

Spiked with rum and spiced with chili powder and mustard, this is an ideal dish for a casual dinner party. Cook the dish the day before you serve it to give the flavors a chance to blend.

■ Drain the beans, place them in a large heavy kettle with the water and oil, and bring just to a boil over high heat. Reduce heat to low, cover the pot, and simmer the beans for 2 hours, or until tender.

While the beans are cooking, form the sausage meat into a flat pattie, place it in a cold skillet, and brown it on one side over moderate heat. Turn the pattie, breaking it up into pieces, and brown on the other side.

Add the sausage, 2 tablespoons of the fat, the onions, garlic and salt, apples, pepper, chili powder, mustard, brown sugar, and tomato juice. Mix gently, bring quickly just to a boil, and reduce the heat. Cover the kettle and simmer the mixture for 2 hours, or until the gravy is thick, or turn the mixture into a casserole and bake in a preheated 325°F oven for 2 hours.

To reheat the beans, preheat the oven to 350°F and bake the casserole for 25 to 30 minutes, or until the bean mixture is bubbling hot.

• 10 to 12 SERVINGS

Five minutes before serving, stir in the rum. Serve with a separate bowl of sour cream.

BAKED KIDNEY
BEANS PROVENÇAL

¼ cup olive oil

1 large Bermuda onion, finely chopped

2 cloves garlic, minced

1 green bell pepper, finely chopped

5 medium tomatoes, peeled, seeded, and chopped

1 bay leaf

½ teaspoon fresh thyme leaves

Salt

Freshly ground black pepper

2 cups cooked red kidney beans

2 tablespoons finely chopped parsley

2½ tablespoons snipped fresh chives

¼ cup freshly grated Parmesan cheese

This is a nice dish to serve in summer, when luscious ripe tomatoes and fresh herbs are easy to find at farm stands or, better yet, in your own garden. The recipe calls for cooked kidney beans, but cannellini (navy) beans, garbanzos, limas, and lentils are all equally tasty prepared in this manner.

■ In a heavy skillet or saucepan heat the oil over moderate heat, add the onion, garlic, and green pepper, and sauté until the onion is translucent. Stir in the tomatoes and simmer for 3 or 4 minutes. Add the bay leaf, and thyme.

Salt and pepper to taste. Cover the pan, and simmer the sauce for 30 minutes.

Preheat the oven to 350°F. Place the beans in a 1½-quart casserole. Pour the tomato sauce over the beans and stir in the parsley and chives. Bake, uncovered, until the liquid has reduced somewhat, about 40 minutes. Sprinkle the top of the casserole with the cheese and bake until the cheese has browned lightly.

• 6 SERVINGS

LEEK AND MUSHROOM PIE WITH KIDNEY BEAN "CRUST"

1½ cups cooked red kidney beans, well drained	2½ cups finely chopped, well-washed whites of leek	1 tablespoon snipped fresh dill or 1 teaspoon dried dill
1 tablespoon unsalted butter or margarine	1½ cups thinly sliced mushrooms	1 teaspoon dry mustard

This protein-packed bean-bottom pie will delight your guests served either as an appetizer or as the main course for a light meal.

■ Pat the beans dry on paper towels, place them between 2 layers of wax paper, and crush them with a rolling pin. Scrape the beans into an 8-inch pie plate and press them all around the bottom and sides to make a crust, just as you would with graham cracker crumbs.

Preheat the oven to 350°F. In a large skillet, melt the butter over moderately low heat, add the leeks, mushrooms, dill, and mustard, and sauté until the leeks are just tender. Remove from heat and cool slightly.

In a mixing bowl, beat the eggs well, add the wine, bread crumbs, Cheddar, and the leek mixture. Stir well and add salt and pepper to taste. Pour the mixture into the pie plate and bake for 30 to 40 minutes, or until the filling is set and browned on top.

¼ cup dry
white wine

3 large eggs

¼ cup bread
crumbs

½ cup shredded
sharp
Cheddar
cheese

Salt

Freshly
ground white
pepper

• 6 to 8
APPETIZER
SERVINGS; 4
MAIN COURSE
SERVINGS

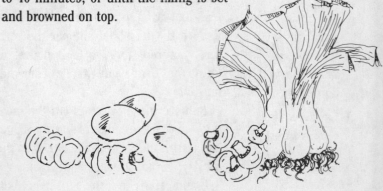

HERBED BEANS, IDAHO STYLE

2 cups dried great northern beans, picked over, rinsed, and soaked

5 cups water

1 teaspoon unsalted butter

1 large meaty ham bone

1 large onion pierced with 2 whole cloves

2 large cloves garlic

1 bay leaf

2 tablespoons finely chopped parsley

1 teaspoon finely chopped fresh winter savory

3 tablespoons pan juices from roast meat or unsalted butter

Salt

Freshly ground parsley

1 teaspoon finely chopped fresh marjoram

1 teaspoon fresh thyme leaves

• 6 SERVINGS

For a perfect meal, serve this dish with a green salad, cornbread sticks, and relishes and follow it with home-made deep-dish fruit pie.

■ Drain the beans, place them in a large, heavy saucepan with the water, butter, ham bone, onion, garlic, and bay leaf, and bring to a boil over high heat. Reduce the heat and simmer the mixture, covered, for 1½ to 2 hours, or until the beans are tender but not mushy.

Remove the ham bone, cut the meat into small pieces, discarding the bone, and return the meat to the pan. Add the parsley, savory, thyme, and pan juices. Salt and pepper to taste. Serve very hot.

NAVY BEANS AND CHUTNEY

■ Drain the beans, place them in a large saucepan with 1 quart of the water, and bring to a boil over high heat. Reduce the heat and simmer the beans, covered, until they are tender, 1½ to 2 hours, adding water as necessary to keep the beans from scorching. Drain the beans and return to the saucepan.

Preheat the oven to 325°F. Add to the beans the bacon, onion, chutney, remaining 1 cup water, mustard, and salt and pepper to taste. Pour the mixture into a shallow 2-quart baking dish and drizzle the honey over the top. Cover the dish and bake the bean mixture for 45 minutes. Remove the cover and bake 30 minutes longer. Serve very hot.

2 cups dried navy beans, picked over, rinsed, and soaked

5 cups water

6 slices bacon, cut into small pieces

1 onion, finely chopped

¼ cup finely chopped chutney

1 cup water

1 teaspoon dry mustard

Salt

Freshly ground black pepper

½ cup honey

• 4 SERVINGS

NAVY BEAN PURÉE

2 cups dried navy beans, picked over, rinsed, and soaked

3 quarts water

1 medium onion, finely chopped

½ teaspoon celery salt

2 teaspoons salt

¼ teaspoon freshly ground black pepper

¼ teaspoon dry mustard

4 tablespoons (½ stick) unsalted butter, cut into 4 pieces and softened

3 hard-cooked eggs, sliced

2 to 3 tablespoons finely chopped parsley

■ Drain the beans, place them in a large kettle with the water and celery salt, and bring to a boil over high heat. Reduce heat and simmer the beans, covered, for about 2 hours, or until very soft.

Drain the beans and purée them coarsely in a food processor or by putting them through the coarse blade of a food mill. Return the beans to the saucepan and stir in the salt, pepper, and mustard. Cook until the mixture thickens to the desired consistency.

Add the butter, 1 piece at a time, stirring until it has melted. Transfer the purée to a heated platter, arrange the sliced eggs around the edge of the platter, and sprinkle the top with the parsley.

• 6 SERVINGS

FRIDAY STEW

This versatile meatless stew can be used as a main course or a side dish, depending on the occasion. The recipe can be expanded simply by doubling the ingredients or, preferably, by adding fresh herbs and other fresh or frozen vegetables, such as cut green beans, green peas, shredded cabbage, sliced zucchini or summer squash, corn kernels, or celery.

■ Drain the beans, place in a large heavy saucepan with cold water to cover, and bring to a boil. Reduce the heat and simmer beans, covered, for about 1½ hours, or until beans are almost tender, adding water as necessary.

While the beans cook, heat the oil in a skillet, add the onions and garlic, and sauté over moderate heat until the onion is translucent. Transfer the onion mixture to the saucepan, add the potatoes, carrots, and tomatoes. Salt and pepper to taste, and add enough water to cover the ingredients. Cook for 30 minutes more, uncovered, or until the potatoes and carrots are tender and the juices are somewhat thickened. Serve in heated soup bowls sprinkled with the parsley.

1 pound dried navy beans, picked over, rinsed, and soaked

½ cup olive or vegetable oil

1 cup finely chopped onions

2 cloves garlic, minced

1 cup diced peeled potatoes

1 cup diced carrots

2 cups canned tomatoes, with juices, chopped

Salt

Freshly ground black pepper

½ cup chopped parsley

• 4 to 6 ENTREE SERVINGS

COWBOY BEANS

2 pounds pinto
beans,
picked over,
rinsed, and
soaked

2 pounds
smoked ham
hocks

1 cup finely
chopped
onion

¼ cup sugar

¼ cup chopped
drained
canned
chiles

1½ cups tomato
purée

Salt

Freshly
ground
pepper

• 6 to 8
SERVINGS

These are about as close to the real thing as you can get this side of the chuck wagon!

■ Drain the beans, place them in a large heavy kettle with cold water to cover, and bring to a boil over high heat. Lower the heat and simmer the beans until they are tender, 1½ to 2 hours, adding water as needed.

Add the ham hock to the kettle and simmer 15 minutes more. Add the onion, sugar, chiles, and tomato purée and cook 15 to 20 minutes longer. Remove the ham hocks and cut the meat into small pieces, discarding the bone. Return the meat to the kettle, stir well, and correct the seasonings. Serve with meat chili, steaks, or other main courses.

PINTO BEAN TOSTADAS

2 tablespoons unsalted butter or margarine

½ cup finely chopped onion

1 tablespoon minced garlic

3 cups cooked pinto beans, drained

Salt

Freshly ground black pepper

3 or 4 large flour tortillas, fried in lard or oil until crisp, then drain

½ cup bean sprouts (mung, alfalfa, lentil, or mixed)

½ cup peeled, seeded, and chopped tomato

1 cup shredded iceberg lettuce

¼ cup thinly sliced pitted black olives

Bottled salsa verde

■ Preheat the oven to 400°F. In a skillet melt the butter over moderate heat, add the onion and garlic, and sauté until the onion is translucent. Add the beans, mix well, and season to taste with salt and pepper.

Place the tortillas on a baking sheet and layer the ingredients on each as follows: the bean-onion mixture, bean sprouts, tomatoes, lettuce, and black olives. Bake the tostadas for 10 minutes, then arrange on heated plates. Pass a bowl of salsa separately.

• 3 or 4
SERVINGS

MAIZE ENCHILADAS

2 tablespoons
vegetable oil

½ cup finely
chopped
onion

1 teaspoon
dried
oregano

½ teaspoon
ground
coriander

½ teaspoon dry
mustard

1½ teaspoons
chili powder

1 cup cooked
pinto beans,
drained

Salt

Freshly
ground
pepper

8 corn tortillas

1½ cups peeled,
seeded, and
diced
tomatoes

1½ cups cooked
whole
kernel corn,
drained

1½ cups grated
Monterey
Jack cheese

1 tablespoon
chopped
fresh
coriander
(cilantro)

■ Preheat the oven to 400°F. Lightly grease 2 large baking sheets.

In a heavy skillet, heat the oil, add the onion, oregano, ground coriander, mustard, and chili powder, and sauté the mixture until the onion is translucent, 3 to 5 minutes. Add the beans and cook until they are heated through, mashing them into the onion mixture. Season to taste with salt and pepper.

Spread the tortillas out on the baking sheets and layer them as follows: the bean mixture, tomatoes, corn, cheese, and fresh coriander. Bake for 5 minutes, or until all the ingredients are heated through and the cheese has melted. Serve at once.

• 4 SERVINGS

JALISCO PIZZAS

SAUCE

- 2 cups peeled, seeded, and chopped tomatoes
- 1 tablespoon minced garlic
- 1½ teaspoons chili powder
- 1 teaspoon dried oregano
- 1 teaspoon ground cumin
- 1 teaspoon paprika
- ½ teaspoon salt

PIZZAS

- 2 tablespoons unsalted butter or margarine
- ½ cup finely chopped onion
- 2 tablespoons minced garlic
- ¼ cup chopped canned green chili peppers
- ¼ cup chopped pitted black olives
- 2 cups refried beans, canned or homemade (page 121)
- Salt
- Freshly ground black pepper
- 8 10-inch corn or flour tortillas
- 3 cups shredded iceberg lettuce
- 3 cups grated Monterey Jack cheese
- 1 cup thinly sliced zucchini
- ¾ cup sour cream

These pizzas are easiest to bake and serve on individual flameproof dishes. But lacking these, simply arrange the tortillas on baking sheets, run them under the broiler, then transfer the pizzas to heated serving plates as soon as the cheese has melted.

■ To make the sauce, place the tomatoes, garlic, chili powder, oregano, cumin, paprika, and salt in a small saucepan and bring to a simmer over moderate heat. Lower heat and simmer the sauce, uncovered, for 15 minutes. Remove the sauce from the heat, transfer to a serving bowl, and cool.

Preheat the broiler. In a heavy skillet, melt the butter over moderate heat, add the onion and garlic, and sauté until the onion is golden. Stir in the chili peppers, olives, and beans and, stirring often, cook until all the ingredients are heated through. Stir in salt and pepper to taste.

Arrange the tortillas on individual flameproof serving dishes or on baking sheets. Spread each tortilla with the following layers: sauce, the refried bean mixture, lettuce, and cheese; then distribute the zucchini slices on top of each "pizza" as if they were pepperoni slices.

Broil the pizzas just until the cheese melts. Place a dollop of sour cream in the center of each pizza and serve at once.

• 6 to 8
SERVINGS

NORTH BEACH PINTO

BEAN PIZZA

2 tablespoons
unsalted
butter or
margarine

½ cup finely
chopped
onion

2 tablespoons
minced garlic

¼ cup finely
chopped
green bell
pepper

1 tablespoon
chopped fresh
rosemary or 1
teaspoon
ground dried
rosemary

2 tablespoons
chopped fresh
oregano or 2
teaspoons
ground dried
oregano

1 cup peeled,
seeded, and
chopped tomato

Salt

Freshly
ground black
pepper

½ cup grated
Provolone
cheese

¼ cup grated
Mozzarella
cheese

½ cup grated
medium
Cheddar cheese

2 tablespoons
freshly grated
Parmesan
cheese

4 to 6 prebaked
individual
pizza crusts

3 cups cooked
pinto beans,
drained

½ cup thinly
sliced Genoa
salami,
pepperoni, or
chorizo

¼ cup thinly
sliced pitted
black olives

¼ cup chopped
parsley

■ Preheat the oven to 450°F. In a skillet, melt the butter over moderate heat, add the onion, garlic, bell pepper, rosemary, and oregano, and sauté until the onion is translucent. Stir in the tomatoes and simmer the mixture for 10 minutes, or until the sauce is thick enough to spread on the pizza crusts without running. Add salt and pepper to taste.

In a bowl or on a sheet of wax paper combine the Provolone, Mozzarella, Cheddar, and Parmesan cheeses. Arrange the pizza crusts on baking sheets. Spread half the tomato sauce over each crust, then divide the pinto beans among the crusts. Spread the remaining sauce over the beans, sprinkle with the cheese mixture, distribute the salami slices over the cheese, and finish with the olives and parsley.

Bake the pizzas until they are heated through and the cheese melts. Serve at once.

• 4 to 6
SERVINGS

SWEET AND

SOUR SOYBEANS

2 tablespoons corn or peanut oil

½ cup diced onion

1 teaspoon minced garlic

½ teaspoon minced fresh ginger (optional)

¼ cup chopped green pepper

½ cup diced carrot

¾ cup fresh or drained canned pineapple chunks

2½ cups cooked soybeans, drained

Salt

Freshly ground black pepper

1½ tablespoons cornstarch

½ cup dark brown sugar

⅓ cup water

1½ tablespoons soy sauce

1½ tablespoons dry sherry

½ cup white wine vinegar

2 tomatoes, peeled, seeded, and cut into wedges

Steamed rice

■ In a large saucepan heat the oil over moderate heat, add the onion, garlic, ginger if desired, green pepper, and carrot, and stir-fry the mixture for 1 minute; the vegetables should still be crisp. Add the pineapple and soybeans and cook, stirring often, until they are heated through and well mixed with the vegetables. Add salt and pepper to taste, remove from the heat, and keep warm.

In a small saucepan combine the

cornstarch and brown sugar. Stir in the water, soy sauce, sherry, and vinegar and bring the mixture to a boil over low heat, stirring constantly. Cook the sauce until it has thickened, but do not overcook.

Pour the sauce into the warm soybean mixture, add the tomato wedges, and stir gently but thoroughly. Serve at once over heated rice.

• 4 to 6
SERVINGS

SOYBEAN LOAF

2 cups cooked soybeans, thoroughly mashed

½ cup dried bread crumbs

2 tablespoons grated onion

4 tablespoons (½ stick) unsalted butter, softened

1 tablespoon celery salt

Freshly ground pepper

2 large eggs, beaten

½ cup milk

½ cup water

Tomato sauce

■ Preheat the oven to 350°F and butter a 1½-quart baking dish. In a mixing bowl, combine the soybeans, bread crumbs, onion, celery salt, black pepper to taste, eggs, milk, and water and blend very well. Transfer the mixture to the baking dish and bake for 25 minutes, uncovered, or until the top is delicately browned. Serve with tomato sauce.

• 6 SERVINGS

BEAN GLOSSARY

BLACK BEANS Also known as turtle beans. Small, kidney-shaped beans with black skins and creamy interiors, often used in a rich, thick soup. Popular in the Southern U.S. and a staple in South American, Caribbean, and Mexican cuisines.

BLACK-EYED BEANS Also known as black-eyed peas and cowpeas. These Southern favorites have a sweet, pealike flavor, a buttery texture, and a singular appearance: a black dot on a yellow skin. Throughout the Southern U.S. they are cooked with ham hocks or other salted meat.

BUTTER BEANS *See* lima beans.

CRANBERRY BEANS Sold fresh or canned, these beans have a sweet, strong flavor and a plump shape similar to cranberries. Used often in Italian cuisine (and sometimes called Roman beans); a favorite for succotash.

FAVA BEANS   Also known as horse beans. They are available fresh in early spring, when their flavor is sweet. Buy only young, bright green beans; those that have yellowed will be too tough. Dried favas, which are popular in Mediterranean countries, have a strong taste and need long soaking. After cooking, they are best puréed, as their skins are usually tough and unpleasant to eat.

GARBANZO BEANS   Also known as chickpeas and ceci. Small, tan beans with a nutlike flavor, garbanzos need long, slow cooking. They appear in a vast range of dishes, from appetizers to soups to main courses to side dishes. The beans are widely used throughout the world and are especially important in the cuisines of India, the Middle East, North Africa, the Mediterranean, and South America.

GREAT NORTHERN BEANS   *See* white beans.

GREEN BEANS   Also known as snap beans, haricots, and string beans. A tender, edible pod with light green seeds, this favorite is the young version of such dried beans as great northerns, navy beans, kidney beans, cannellini, and small white beans. Green beans are available fresh and frozen year round.

ITALIAN GREEN BEANS   A broad, green bean, occasionally available fresh in summer and frozen year round. Sauté quickly in butter or olive oil with garlic and tomatoes and use as a side dish.

KIDNEY BEANS   Kidney-shaped and brownish-red in color, these familiar beans are the mature seeds of a variety of green beans. They are closely related to pinto and pink beans and are kissing cousins of navy beans, great northerns, and other white beans. Kidney beans can be used for just about any course except dessert.

LENTILS   Not a bean, but another kind of legume, lentils are the biblical pottage for which Esau sold his birthright. Available only in their dried form, they are delicately but distinctively flavored. Lentils need no soaking, only sorting over to pick out any debris and then a quick rinse. Cook lentils gently, watching closely toward the end of cooking to see that they do not disintegrate.

LIMA BEANS   Also known as butter beans. Among the varieties are Fordhook and several other large beans and baby limas, which of course are smaller. Both large and small beans are available fresh in season, frozen, and dried. Among dried limas, the larger variety has a distinctive nutlike flavor that sets it apart from all other beans. Fresh limas are one of the key ingredients of succotash.

MUNG BEANS   Small beans native to India, mung beans are grown extensively in the Orient where they are eaten whole or used for bean sprouts. In the U.S., the sprouts are sold fresh or canned.

NAVY BEANS   *See* white beans.

PEAS   Peas are another very ancient legume with a long recorded history. Green peas are available in the shell or frozen. Dried green and yellow split peas, like lentils, need no soaking and cook quickly. Dried split pea soup made with a ham bone and a few aromatic vegetables is one of the great comforts of northern winters.

PINK BEANS A close relative of the kidney bean; popular for Mexican dishes.

PINTO BEANS A mottled pink and brown bean, still another variety of kidney bean, and also used in Mexican cuisine.

RED BEANS A favorite for chili, three-bean salad, and casseroles, this is another kidney bean variety.

SNAP BEANS A variety of green bean.

SOLDIER BEANS A medium-size dried white bean with a sweet flavor and a reddish center; used by New Englanders for baked beans.

SOYBEANS Round beans with a crisp, nutlike flavor, these seeds are processed into oil, flour, and milk. Soybeans were introduced into the United States in 1804, but they became a large-scale crop only in 1924. There are many varieties and many hundreds of types and strains are known, but basically the beans can be classified as either commercial field-type or edible vegetable-type. The commercial field varieties are suited for the production of oil, oil meal, and flour, while the edible varieties are dried and used for cooking in the home.

WHITE BEANS All the mature seeds of one variety or another of green bean, this group includes navy beans, great northern yankee beans, cannellini, white kidney beans, and small white beans.

WINGED BEANS Winged beans were "discovered" in 1974 in the United States by the National Academy of

Sciences. Called "a supermarket on a stalk" by scientists who have been testing it, the winged bean apparently combines the best characteristics of both the green bean and the pea and also includes some traits of spinach, mushrooms, soybeans, potatoes, and bean sprouts. According to scientists, the bean is chockful of minerals, vitamins, protein, fiber, and complex carbohydrates as well as other essential nutrients.

Almost all of the bean is edible, and the flowers, leaves, tender new shoots, seeds, and tuberous roots can easily be digested by human beings. Only the stalk is disposable from both a culinary and nutritional standpoint. At present the bean is being grown in tropical climates, but it has the potential to grow in many different kinds of soil and in more moderate climates provided they are not too severely cold. We are all awaiting the advent of this undoubted lifesaver to the list of foods grown worldwide.

YELLOW WAX BEANS   A variety of green beans.

YANKEE BEANS   *See* white beans.

INDEX

ABOUT THE AUTHOR

F. H. "Ted" Waskey is a Certified Executive Chef, a Registered and Licensed Dietitian, and the holder of a doctorate in Administration. A Master Craftsman in the Craft Guild of Chefs, he is a member of The Royal Cookery and Food Society in the U.K., a Fellow of the American Academy of Chefs, a Certified Hotel Administrator, a Certified Culinary Educator, a Fellow of the Society for the Advancement of Food Research, and a professional member of both The Institute of Food Technologists and The Food Consultants Society International.

Dr. Waskey is currently the Senior Professor in Food Management and Nutrition and Coordinator, Graduate Studies, at the Conrad N. Hilton College of Hotel and Restaurant Management at the University of Houston, where he also maintains an active consulting practice and writes for a number of scientific and trade journals.